ANCIENT ROME

A Comprehensive Resource
for the Active Study of Ancient Rome

DECEM
MARS
VIGILA
PEDES
GLADIUS
NAVIS
DOMUS
TEPIDARIUM
VOLUMEN
VALE

Written by George Moore

Published by World Teachers Press®

Published with the permission of R.I.C. Publications Pty. Ltd.

First published by R.I.C. Publications Pty. Ltd., Perth, Western Australia. Revised by Didax Educational Resources.

Printed in the United States of America.

Order Number 2-5175
ISBN 1-58324-109-4

D E F G H I 07 06 05 04 03

Educational Resources
395 Main Street
Rowley, MA 01969
www.worldteacherspress.com

Foreword

From its beginning in the 8th century B.C. to the fall of the Western Empire in the 5th century A.D., the Roman Empire lasted over 1,200 years, outlasting all other empires. Professor John Wacher, a leading authority on the history of Rome, believes it was one of the "most influential empires of all time."

Rome's huge empire surrounded the Mediterranean Sea, extending from the Sahara Desert to the River Rhine in northern Europe, and from Spain in the west to Syria in the east.

The fascinating story of Rome from its beginning as a tiny group of villages in the hills to an empire that ruled the known world, and then its subsequent decline, has enthralled historians for hundreds of years. Even when the barbarians brought about the disintegration of the Empire, many aspects of the Roman civilization had an enormous influence on the cultures that followed. The ideas passed on were not just Roman but ideas and literature the Romans gathered from other ancient cultures. Many early Greek writings are only available to modern experts because the Romans made copies of them.

Under Rome's control, all the countries in the Empire were united for the only time in their history, a testimony to the influence of the Romans on the world of that time.

The Roman Empire is one of the greatest success stories in history and well worthy of study by the students in our schools.

Contents

TEACHER'S NOTES

Ancient Rome provides you with an in-depth review of this ancient civilization, presented through text, pictorial representation and a wide range of written and oral activities.

Written Activities

Activities include a wide range of learning areas and strategies. The presentation of informational text provides ideal opportunity for use within a language program, while the content is suited to studies of society and history. This mix is an ideal resource to promote cross-curricula learning. Activity types include:

- comprehension
- literature study
- sequencing
- cloze
- mapping
- matching
- arts and crafts
- puzzles
- debating

Oral Activities

The story of Ancient Rome is a fascinating one that provides ideal motivation for small group and whole class discussion. Many opportunities are identified throughout this book for discussion to occur on the different aspects of life in Roman times. These discussions are ideally done in a comparative model with the students' daily life. Use of the other two books in this series, *Ancient Egypt* and *Ancient Greece* also provides opportunities for comparative discussions and studies.

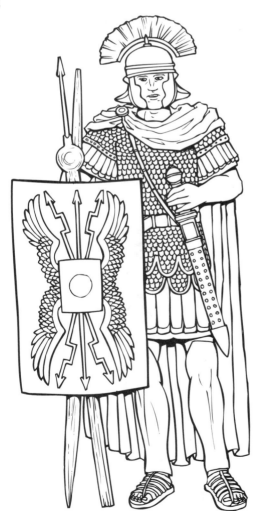

Teacher's Notes

Teacher's Notes are provided for each activity. This includes detailed information that provides you with a greater level of background information in order to promote and assist discussion on the topic. These pages are also presented in a manner where the student can use the page as additional information and further activities can be developed on this text.

At the bottom of this page, additional activities are suggested where appropriate.

Activity Pages

Provide detailed information on the aspect of Ancient Rome being studied. This text is provided in sufficient detail for discussion to occur in small or whole class groups. Each passage of text/ information is accompanied by an activity as outlined above.

TEACHER'S NOTES

FOUNDATION OF ROME

The Etruscans were skilful seamen who traded with Greece, North Africa, Egypt and the Near East. Their language was different from other languages in the Western Mediterranean and little is known about their origins. They ruled much of Italy for 300 years before their defeat by more powerful Roman legions.

Scholars don't know much about the structure of the Etruscan language, which doesn't resemble Greek or Latin. In the 19th century an Etruscan document was found in the wrappings of an Egyptian mummy, but philologists have still been unable to find a key to the language. The discovery of the Rosetta stone unlocked the mysteries of Egyptian hieroglyphics and scholars are hoping for a similar find for the Etruscan language. In 1964, three gold tablets were excavated near Rome. They contained Etruscan and Punic inscriptions, but despite months examining and comparing them, scholars found there was insufficient information to provide any new knowledge.

As the Roman Empire spread from its humble beginnings, conquered countries became provinces controlled by governors. Roman conquest brought improved legal systems (our civil laws are developed from Roman law), better farming methods, splendid roads and buildings, but also brutality. Cicero, a famous orator and politician, was critical of this aspect of the Empire when he wrote, "There isn't a place which has not been invaded by the greed and injustice of our fellow Romans ... it is hard to find words to say how much foreign nations hate us".

The Empire began in 27 B.C. with the rule of the Emperor Augustus. Despite the disadvantages of living under Roman rule it is important to remember that Latin, the Roman language, has formed the basis of modern languages such as Italian, English, French, Spanish and Portuguese.

Activity Suggestions

When the early Romans drove out Rome's last king, Tarquin, the Etruscan leader, Lars Porsena, supported Tarquin and attacked Rome. The bridge leading into the city across the Tiber was defended by the Roman hero, Horatius. Though Lars Porsena ruled Rome for a few years, historians believe Horatius is a legendary person.

Read and discuss Lord Macaulay's poem about Horatius in his book "Lays of Ancient Rome."

Teacher's Notes

Additional information provided for the teacher can also be used by students for additional information and activity.

Suggested Activity

Include a variety of activities to be used for further development of the topic.

Topic Text

Text and illustrations provide a solid base of information on the topic being studied.

Activity

A wide variety of activities are provided to develop the study of the topic.

FOUNDATION OF ROME

Archaeologists believe the mighty Roman Empire started before 1000 B.C. It probably began as a small cluster of wooden huts on the hills near the River Tiber on the west coast of central Italy. As the settlement, built on fertile farmland, grew in size and population, the powerful kingdom of Etruria to its north became interested. Soon they took control of the region and built the city of Rome.

The Etruscans were religious, artistic people who produced fine paintings, ceramics and sculptures. They traveled widely and traded with far-off lands while the Romans were just simple farmers. Seven kings ruled Rome until 509 B.C. when Roman nobles led the people and drove out the last Etruscan king, Tarquin. The nobles then declared Rome was a republic where its citizens would elect their rulers. The Romans gradually conquered most of Italy, including the Greeks who had settled in the south. At the height of its power the Roman Empire stretched from Britain to the Middle East and included 80 million people of all nationalities.

Activity Box

1. What helped the original settlement to grow? _____

2. Who was the last ruler of the Etruscans? _____

3. How does a republic benefit its citizens? _____

4. In which part of Italy were the Greek settlements? _____

5. What outer boundaries of the Empire were mentioned? _____

6. Why do you think the Etruscans became interested in the original settlement of Rome? _____

_____

7. In one sentence describe the Estruscan people.

_____

_____

FOUNDATION OF ROME

The Etruscans were skillful seamen who traded with Greece, North Africa, Egypt and the Near East. Their language was different from other languages in the Western Mediterranean and little is known about their origins. They ruled much of Italy for 300 years before their defeat by more powerful Roman legions.

Scholars don't know much about the structure of the Etruscan language, which doesn't resemble Greek or Latin. In the 19th century an Etruscan document was found in the wrappings of an Egyptian mummy, but philologists have still been unable to find a key to the language. The discovery of the Rosetta stone unlocked the mysteries of Egyptian hieroglyphics and scholars are hoping for a similar find for the Etruscan language. In 1964, three gold tablets were excavated near Rome. They contained Etruscan and Punic inscriptions, but despite months examining and comparing them, scholars found there was insufficient information to provide any new knowledge.

As the Roman Empire spread from its humble beginnings, conquered countries became provinces controlled by governors. Roman conquest brought improved legal systems (our civil laws are developed from Roman law), better farming methods, splendid roads and buildings, but also brutality. Cicero, a famous orator and politician, was critical of this aspect of the Empire when he wrote, "There isn't a place which has not been invaded by the greed and injustice of our fellow Romans ... it is hard to find words to say how much foreign nations hate us."

The Empire began in 27 B.C. with the rule of the Emperor Augustus. Despite the disadvantages of living under Roman rule it is important to remember that Latin, the Roman language, has formed the basis of modern languages such as Italian, English, French, Spanish and Portuguese.

Activity Suggestions

When the early Romans drove out Rome's last king, Tarquin, the Etruscan leader, Lars Porsena, supported Tarquin and attacked Rome. The bridge leading into the city across the Tiber was defended by the Roman hero, Horatius. Though Lars Porsena ruled Rome for a few years, historians believe Horatius is a legendary person.

Read and discuss Lord Macaulay's poem about Horatius in his book "Lays of Ancient Rome."

FOUNDATION OF ROME

Archaeologists believe the mighty Roman Empire started before 1000 B.C. It probably began as a small cluster of wooden huts on the hills near the River Tiber on the west coast of central Italy. As the settlement, built on fertile farmland, grew in size and population, the powerful kingdom of Etruria to its north became interested. Soon the Etruscans took control of the region and built the city of Rome.

The Etruscans were religious, artistic people who produced fine paintings, ceramics and sculptures. They traveled widely and traded with far-off lands while the Romans were just simple farmers. Seven kings ruled Rome until 509 B.C. when Roman nobles led the people and drove out the last Etruscan king, Tarquin. The nobles then declared Rome was a republic where its citizens would elect their rulers. The Romans gradually conquered most of Italy, including the Greeks who had settled in the south. At the height of its power the Roman Empire stretched from Britain to the Middle East and included 80 million people of many nationalities.

Activity Box

1. What helped the original settlement to grow? _____
   _____

2. Who was the last ruler of the Etruscans? _____

3. How does a republic benefit its citizens? _____

4. In which part of Italy were the Greek settlements? _____

5. What outer boundaries of the Empire were mentioned? _____

6. Why do you think the Etruscans became interested in the original settlement of Rome?
   _____
   _____

7. In one sentence describe the Estruscan people.
   _____
   _____

FOUNDATION OF ROME (2)

See page 16 for Foundation of Rome background information and teacher's notes.

Activity Suggestions

Discuss how climatic conditions appeared to direct the spread of the Roman Empire. Identify the climate types at the different borders of the empire and explain how these climate types would have prevented the further spread of the empire.

Identify the physical barriers preventing the spread of the empire.

Construct a map showing the climatic and physical barriers which controlled the spread of the Roman Empire.

FOUNDATION OF ROME (2)

8. Use an atlas and write the modern names of conquered countries in the Roman Empire next to their ancient names.

    Macedonia • • _____

    Cyrenaica • • _____

    Cappadocia • • _____

    Gallia • • _____

    Britannia • • _____

    Hispania • • _____

    Numidia • • _____

    Thracia • • _____

9. Using your atlas, suggest reasons why the Roman empire did not spread further south into Africa and further north into what is now called northern and eastern Europe.

    _____

    _____

    _____

ROMULUS AND REMUS

This well-known Roman legend, written during the first century B.C., is about the founding of Rome. It was written by a Roman historian called Livy, whose books were often an interesting mixture of legend and facts.

The Roman god Mars is mentioned only briefly in the story, for the Romans, unlike the Greeks, did not favor legends about their gods. Their stories were about the Romans themselves—their heroes, early Roman history and family relationships.

Activity Suggestions

The city of Rome is on the River Tiber. Give students a related homework/library exercise (using atlases or the Internet) to find out which rivers flow through these famous cities:

(a) Paris	(b) New York	(c) London	(d) Cairo	(e) Melbourne
(f) Washington	(g) Cambridge	(h) Lisbon	(i) Quebec	(j) Dublin

Answers:

(a) Seine	(b) Hudson	(c) Thames	(d) Nile	(e) Yarra
(f) Potomac	(g) Cam	(h) Tagus	(i) St. Lawrence	(j) Liffey

ROMULUS AND REMUS

This Roman legend tells of the founding of Rome by a soldier-farmer called Romulus.

Two brothers, Amulius and Numitor, quarreled over who should be ruler and eventually the younger Amulius made himself king. He banished Numitor from the kingdom and then killed his brother's sons. Later, Amulius ordered his brother's pretty daughter, Rhea Sylvia, not to marry or have children. Amulius feared any children she might have would seek revenge against him for his terrible deed. However, Rhea had twin sons, Romulus and

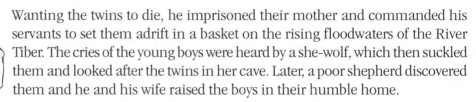

Remus, and declared that Mars, the Roman god of war, was their father. Amulius was furious.

Wanting the twins to die, he imprisoned their mother and commanded his servants to set them adrift in a basket on the rising floodwaters of the River Tiber. The cries of the young boys were heard by a she-wolf, which then suckled them and looked after the twins in her cave. Later, a poor shepherd discovered them and he and his wife raised the boys in their humble home.

When they were adults, the boys were told how Amulius had tried to drown them. Seeking revenge, they slew Amulius and placed their grandfather, Numitor, on the throne. The brothers then decided to build a new city but quarreled over its location. Following what he believed was a sign from the gods which favored him, Romulus decided to build the city on the site he had chosen. This angered Remus and during another fierce argument Romulus killed Remus and then began building the city of Rome.

Activity Box

1. Who was Rome named after in legend?

   _____

2. Who was Rhea Sylvia's father?

   _____

3. In a legend there is usually a hero and a villain. Who was the villain in this story?

   _____

4. Explain the phrase "their humble home" in your own words.

   _____

   _____

   _____

5. What was Amulius's "terrible deed"?

   _____

   _____

   _____

6. Why do you think Rhea said that Mars was her sons' father?

   _____

   _____

7. Give synonyms from the passage for these words:

   (a) irate _____

   (b) exiled _____

   (c) killed _____

8. Name the twins mentioned in the legend.

   _____

9. Two words in the passage that mean "instructed" are:

   _____

10. Circle the correct answer.
    Amulius was the...

    uncle   **brother**   **grandfather**

    nephew   **great uncle**   ...of Remus.

ROMULUS AND REMUS (2)

The city of Rome is thought to have begun in a small village in a region of Italy called Latium. Roman legends adopted from the Greeks also tell us that the ancient Romans believed they could trace their ancestry back to a person called Aeneas, a hero who escaped from the complete destruction of the city of Troy (Ilium) by the Greeks. The legend reinforced the hero aspect favored by the Romans by saying that Aeneas carried his father on his back in the escape. Aeneas later moved on to Carthage before finally deciding to settle in Latium.

Aeneas eventually had a son who founded the city of Alba Longa and the legend tells us that Romulus and Remus, traditional founders of Rome, were descended from the kings of Alba Longa. During the last 10 years of his life, the famous Roman poet, Virgil, wrote his epic poem "Aeneid," a poem in 12 books which retold the legend of Aeneas and outlined the growth of the Roman Empire.

The legend of Romulus and Remus may be partially true, for we know that two villages, one on the Palatine Hill, merged to form a single settlement in the 8th century B.C. This was around 753 B.C.—the date recognized in legend. However, the discovery at the beginning of the 20th century of hut foundations and burial sites on the Palatine Hill cast doubts on the veracity of the foundation story. Archaeologists decided that some of the burial sites dated back to the 10th century B.C., hundreds of years before the legend of Romulus and Remus.

In what is believed to be another early foundation legend, Romulus invited his powerful enemies, the Sabines, to a feast and during the celebrations the Romans seized the Sabine women for their wives.

Ancient Rome

ROMULUS AND REMUS (2)

Activity Box

Complete the crossword puzzle. All answers are in the legend of Romulus and Remus.

Clues

Across

3. Action
5. A quarrel
8. Monarch
9. Angry
10. Informed
13. Commenced
14. Vengeance
15. A powerful being
16. Reared
18. Erect
19. Killed

Down

1. Conflict
2. Youthful
3. Perish
4. Selected
6. Royal chair
7. Ordered
10. Attempted
11. Myth
12. Annoyed
17. Location

DESTRUCTION OF POMPEII

Tacitus had inquired about the death of Pliny the Elder, Uncle of Pliny the Younger and commander of a Roman fleet. Pliny the Elder, an asthmatic, had died at Stabiae when he tried to save friends while on a rescue mission to help the people of Pompeii. The 56-year-old's ships could not reach the shore because of falling debris, and carried on to Stabiae.

The ruins at Pompeii were first stumbled upon accidentally by an architect in the 16th century as he tunneled under the ground as part of a plan to take water to a nearby town. Not recognizing the site's importance, he did little to follow up the find. The eruption had changed the landscape of the region so much that, in later years, location of the original site of Pompeii would have been very difficult. The course of the Sarno River had been changed and the beach on the Tyrrhenian Sea raised so much that major changes had taken place.

Excavations at Pompeii began in 1748 after a peasant digging in a local vineyard struck a wall below the surface of the ground. King Charles III, then ruler of the kingdom around the present city of Naples, was excited by the discovery and was there when excavations began. Unfortunately, those people involved in the early digs were mainly hunting for valuable objects. There was no systematic planning and no careful recording of objects found or their location. Despite interruptions through wars and political troubles, excavations are still being carried out today. Though wooden objects have rotted away over the centuries, archaeologists have discovered much about life in Roman times from the many marble, ceramic, bronze and silver artifacts which have survived.

DESTRUCTION OF POMPEII

Stepping stones in a Pompeii street with gaps for chariot wheels.

Mount Vesuvius, about 1.5 km from Pompeii, erupted on August 24 in 79 A.D. It destroyed the ancient trading town of Pompeii and nearby towns, Stabiae and Herculaneum. The eruption carried ash to the African coast about 1,000 km away. An eyewitness account has been preserved in letters by Pliny the Younger to the Roman historian, Tacitus. Pliny wrote that he and his mother were "enveloped in night ... only the shrill cries of women, the wailing of children, the shouting of men could be heard."

Pompeii was covered with small fragments of volcanic rock (lapilli) and ash to a depth of 7 meters. This covering sealed the town and preserved a remarkable and most important archaeological site. About 17 years earlier, Pompeii and Herculaneum had suffered a strong earthquake but the inhabitants had returned to rebuild their homes.

Many residents of Pompeii died because they inhaled poisonous sulfur fumes. Organic matter was often turned into carbon by the intense heat. In a temple built to the goddess Isis, a partly eaten meal of eggs, fish and nuts was still lying on a table where it had been left by priests fleeing from the destruction.

In time, survivors returned to the devastated site to dig out valuables and other personal possessions. About 2,000 victims from Pompeii's population of approximately 20,000 have been unearthed since excavations began in 1748.

The town of Pompeii has been buried under the hardened ash for 1,900 years. More human and animal remains and artifacts are expected to be discovered as excavations continue today.

Activity Box

Answer these questions on the passage above.

1. Pompeii suffered an earthquake around

   _____.

2. Why is Pompeii an important archaeological site?

   _____

3. What percentage of Pompeii's population has been unearthed?

   _____

4. Which phrase tells us that Pliny was there at the time?

   _____

5. Why did survivors of the eruption return to the site?

   _____

   _____

6. Apart from ash and rocks, what else killed Pompeii's citizens?

   _____

7. How many years have passed since the Pompeii eruption of Mt. Vesuvius?

   _____

8. Give synonyms from the passage for these words:

   (a) residents _____

   (b) high-pitched _____

   (c) toxic _____

   (d) location _____

   (e) interred _____

EXCAVATIONS AT POMPEII

Giuseppe Fiorella organized his excavation workers so nothing was left to chance. He made records of all discoveries and, for a time, they were left where they were found on the site for further examination. A detailed plan of the site was drawn and the exact location of each find was recorded on it. His plan divided the town into regions, which were numbered. Within those regions the insulae (blocks of houses like our modern apartments) were also numbered. Because he was so careful and methodical, scholars were able to find out what buildings had been used for and who had lived in them. He also devised a method of entering buildings from above to prevent the walls collapsing.

Fiorella's most famous innovation was his idea of filling underground cavities with liquid plaster. When the plaster solidified it took an impression of what had once caused the cavity. This was usually a body or a wooden item, both of which had decomposed over the centuries.

Activity Suggestion

Have students write notes and illustrate another disaster which has caused devastation and loss of life like Pompeii, e.g., the *Titanic*, Krakatoa, Great Fire of London, the San Francisco earthquake, Chernobyl, the *Hindenburg*, or the bubonic plague.

EXCAVATIONS AT POMPEII

From 1861, the Italian authorities treated the discovery of Pompeii more seriously, for much damage had been done by previous excavations. It is now regarded as one of the most important archaeological sites because its ruins are so well preserved. Giuseppe Fiorella, a man from nearby Naples, was appointed Chief Archaeologist and he introduced new methods at the digs.

Cut out the boxes and glue in correct order on another sheet of paper.

Hot wet ash

The dead body is soon covered with layers of ash and stones.

When the plaster solidifies, it can be dug carefully out of the soil.

The surface soil is cleared and when a cavity is detected the archaeologist carefully drills a narrow shaft down to it.

Ash and pumice stones (solidified lava) rain down on a fleeing victim soon to be overcome by poisonous fumes.

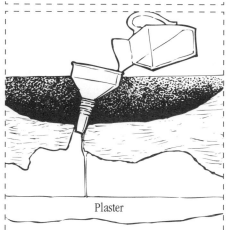

Plaster

Liquid plaster is then poured in to fill the cavity.

Build-up of soil over centuries

Hardened ash

Decayed body leaves a hollow shape

The depth of soil above the cavity deepens as the years pass.

Activity Box

Fiorella's Method

1. Find a strong cardboard box and an irregularly shaped balloon.
2. Mix sand and cement powder with water in proportions that won't set too hard.
3. Inflate the balloon and place it in the cardboard box.
4. Pour the mixture over the balloon so a small piece of the balloon can be seen protruding out of the mixture.
5. Allow the mixture to harden.
6. Prick the exposed part of the balloon with a pin so it deflates.
7. Poor in some liquid plaster and allow it to set hard.
8. Carefully dig away the cement mixture (as Fiorella did) which represents the soil. What did you find?

ROMAN LEGIONS (1)

We know much about the armor worn by legionaries from excavations, particularly the well-preserved finds from Corbridge, once a Roman fort in the north of England. Other information comes from relief carvings on Trajan's column.

Apart from his weapons, a soldier also carried tools for digging fortifications around temporary camps. He also carried personal possessions, such as a mess tin for his food. A legionary was responsible for his weapons and if he lost them he had to pay for new ones.

At the start of each year in Rome, the strongest men in an approximate age range of 25—50 were selected for the army by senior military officers called Tribunes. The Praetorian Guard, a force of about 10,000 men, were special soldiers who were responsible for protecting the emperor, though at times they overthrew an emperor and replaced him.

The Auxiliaries in the Roman army (who carried oval shields) were captured soldiers from conquered nations and were often used for their special skills (such as Syrian archers, slingers from Crete and cavalry from Spain). However, the legionaries had to be citizens of Rome for they were the backbone of the legions and their loyalty to Rome was paramount.

When not fighting, soldiers built bridges, roads and walls to keep out hostile tribes.

Sometimes, when attacking walled cities or heavily armed opponents, Roman soldiers would hold their shields overlapping edge to edge over their heads and down their sides (a testudo—"tortoise") to deflect arrows, spears and rocks fired by the enemy.

ROMAN LEGIONS (1)

Match the correct labels to the diagram.

Woolen leggings were worn in the colder regions of the Empire.

Iron-headed javelin about 2 meters long.

Leather sandals with hobnails on the soles to strengthen them and reduce wear.

Knife on his belt for hand-to-hand combat at close quarters.

Helmet made with leather and bronze (a mixture of mainly copper and tin) strengthened with additions made of iron.

Armor — metal plates hinged with metal or laced together with leather thonging.

Groin guard of leather and metal.

Short sword for thrusting and slashing enemy soldiers.

Metal leg-protectors known as "greaves" were also worn.

Long, curved wooden shield with metal stud in center and metal reinforcement around the edges.

Activity Box

A long curved shield (scutum) was used for centuries until replaced by oval shields or small round ones. Follow the procedure and make your own shield.

1. Work in a group of three—allocate tasks.

2. Obtain a rectangular piece of cardboard (about 50 cm x 35 cm) from school supplies or a supermarket carton.

3. Paint the front of the shield with thick paint. Use string or elastic to hold the curved shape while the paint dries.

4. Decide on your own design and how to show the metal boss on the shield (perhaps half of an old tennis ball, painted or covered with foil).

5. Use paint, colored tape, or cut-out designs in metal foil. Complete your design.

6. Use aluminum foil for the metal edging which the Romans used to strengthen their shields.

    Your teacher will show you how to use the shields you have made to form a testudo.

ROMAN LEGIONS (2)

A common feature of the Roman army was the training. The soldiers practiced constantly as individuals with different types of weapons such as the javelin (pilum) and a short cut-and-thrust sword (gladius), which was a legionary's main weapon. A soldier carried two javelins, a light one and a heavy one, which could pierce shields up to 2.5 cm thick. It had a long metal sheath which prevented an opponent from breaking the shaft. Javelins, which were thrown, were designed to bend on impact so they could not be thrown back by enemy soldiers. The sword blade was about 50 cm long and used to stab and slash an enemy at short range.

A soldier's armor consisted of small plates of bronze linked together and sewn onto leather padding. Later, armor was linked at the top and bottom as well as the sides so that upward thrusts couldn't pierce the armor as they did when the plates were only linked horizontally. This type of armor was easier to produce than chain mail but movement was more restricted.

Though the Romans can't be credited with mixing other metals and carbon with iron to make steel, they were the first to use the harder metal. Their steel-bladed sword helped their legions to conquer much of the known world.

The kingdoms they conquered were allowed to rule themselves as Roman provinces, but if they rebelled against Rome at a later time they would then be destroyed.

ROMAN LEGIONS (2)

In 390 B.C., Celtic warriors from the north swept down through Italy and crushed the Roman army which was defending Rome. In these early days of the republic the Roman army was made up of volunteers. The wild Celts seriously damaged the city and left only after being offered large quantities of gold.

After this humiliating defeat, the Roman army began a period of training and tactical organization which lasted for one hundred years. It gradually became a superb fighting force, one of the best equipped and disciplined armies the world has ever seen. The next time the Romans met the Celts in battle, the tribal warriors were slaughtered by a very professional army of fighting men. Many of the warrior armies the legions faced as the Empire spread lacked this organization, for their leaders were more interested in personal glory.

Apart from being disciplined, the Roman legionaries were extremely fit, for their training program included marching long distances with heavy loads. The Roman infantry (foot soldiers) often covered many kilometers in long campaigns.

Legionary practicing swordsmanship – striking a post at various points with accuracy and force.

Activity Box

1. Why did the Celts win so easily in 390 B.C.? _____

   _____

2. Why did the Celts finally leave Rome? _____

3. What made the later Roman armies so strong? _____

4. The Celts defeated the Romans the next time they met in battle. True or False? _____

5. Who was more interested in personal glory? _____

6. Give another name for the Roman infantry. _____

7. Which word tells us the Roman volunteer army was well beaten? _____

8. How long did the Roman training program last? _____

9. Who were the legionaries? _____

10. What made the Roman soldiers so fit? _____

ROMAN LEGIONS (3)

After Rome defeated the armies of Macedonia around 200 B.C., captured Greek physicians often accompanied Roman armies on military campaigns. The Greeks had a medical tradition dating back to the time of Hypocrites, who lived between 460 B.C. and 370 B.C. Through experiments with animals, the Greeks learned how to set broken bones and heal wounds.

In various parts of Britain, archaeologists have discovered some of the world's first hospitals. They had excellent plumbing and sewerage systems designed for good hygiene; some even had flushing toilets where water carried away waste products. The Romans believed "the smell of excrement" was a source of disease. The hospital buildings were divided into separate wards, probably to isolate infectious diseases.

Their excellent engineering skills no doubt prevented serious epidemics, for in those times more people died from disease than from wounds on the battlefields of the Empire.

The work done by the "medic" on the battlefields added to Roman medical knowledge for there was much practical experience to be gained treating thousands of wounded soldiers and practicing simple surgical procedures. Eventually, medical personnel were attached to all military units, the Roman army being the first military force to have medical units on the battlefield.

ROMAN LEGIONS (3)

Soldiers being treated at a military hospital — shown on Trajan's column in Rome. Trajan was a Spaniard and the first Roman Emperor from one of Rome's conquered countries.

Rome built an empire with its superb armies, but it wasn't just their weapons and training making it possible. The Romans realized that healthy men meant stronger soldiers. They learned much about medicine from the conquered, more cultured Greeks, who were aware of the importance of rest in the recovery process of soldiers wounded in battle. The Romans used simple surgical tools and drugs and set up hospitals in military camps throughout the Empire. Sickness in Rome was dealt with in the home but this care was not available in military camps in remote corners of the Empire, so some of the world's first hospitals were built in the most unlikely places. A battle scene depicted on a Roman monument shows a "doctor" (medicus) bandaging the wounds of a fallen legionary, for the ordinary soldiers were also cared for. These men weren't trained doctors but experienced soldiers who had gained valuable medical skills during their many years in the legions.

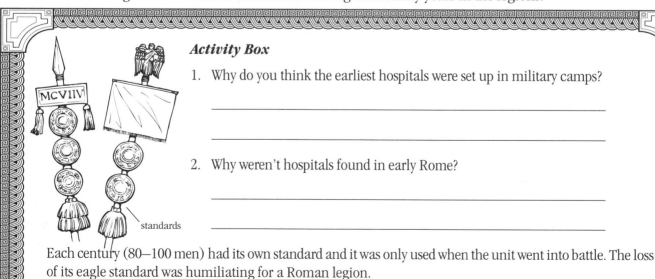

Activity Box

1. Why do you think the earliest hospitals were set up in military camps?

   _____

   _____

2. Why weren't hospitals found in early Rome?

   _____

   _____

standards

Each century (80–100 men) had its own standard and it was only used when the unit went into battle. The loss of its eagle standard was humiliating for a Roman legion.

Make your own standard with a partner. Use paper picnic plates and rectangular pieces of cardboard. Decorate them with paint, colored paper and aluminum foil. An old broom handle will do for the shaft.

ROMAN LEGIONS (4)

After 20 years' service, a legionary was granted a pension and some land, and perhaps a small villa. Captured soldiers from overseas (auxiliaries) who had served Rome well were granted Roman citizenship. Worthy slaves were given their freedom and became free men.

A legion was about 6,000 men. There were ten units called "cohorts" in a legion and six centuries led by a centurion in each cohort. A century originally contained 100 men, but later centuries had only 80. As they faced the enemy, the front line of a legion could be over one kilometer wide and have a depth of 100 to 200 meters. They would have been a formidable and confronting sight for an opposing army.

If a Roman unit retreated it was decimated. This meant every tenth legionary was killed, whereas courageous soldiers received gifts.

For 1,000 years (500 B.C.—500 A.D. approx.), the Roman armies were continually at war, either in the early Roman republic or in provinces of the Empire. Such was their reputation, one Greek writer of those times wrote that Roman generals only wanted men "who will hold their ground when outnumbered ... and die at their posts."

A battle formation:

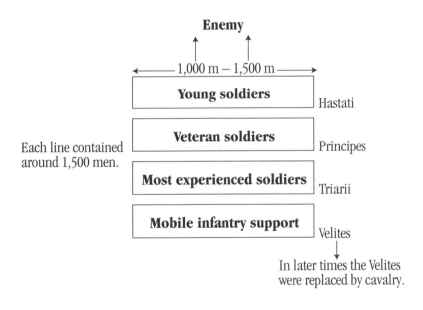

Roman soldiers would often attack in a wedge formation to force a breakthrough in enemy ranks. The Hastati carried hastae (spears) and the Triarii only fought if the battle was being lost. The Velites were the youngest, least able soldiers.

ROMAN LEGIONS (4)

Infantry	Cavalry	Slingers	Archers	Hastati
The foot soldiers.	Fought on horses.	Used slings to throw missiles.	Fought with bows and arrows.	Soldiers who carried a hastae (thrusting spear).

Apart from their weapons, many soldiers and slaves carried tools which were used to build roads, fortifications at temporary camps and bridges to cross rivers quickly in order to surprise the enemy. The Romans, the ancient world's greatest road builders, built straight roads so their armies could move quickly to any trouble spots around the Empire. Often they would clear vegetation from the road verges to prevent ambushes. Their first roads linked their military camps (castra) which gradually developed into towns like Lancaster and Doncaster in England. Excavated Roman roads around the world are often found to be in excellent condition and some modern roads in Britain, like the A5, are actually built on top of old Roman roads. The Roman soldiers and craftsmen who accompanied the legions also built walls and forts to protect the outlying borders of the Empire from warlike tribes.

The A5 main road which was built over Watling Street, probably Britain's oldest Roman road. Notice how straight it is, a visual feature of Roman roads.

Activity Box

1. Who built the Roman roads? _____

2. What was the common feature of Roman roads? _____

3. Name the Roman road mentioned on this page. _____

4. Color and cut out these pictures of fighting men and paste them in the correct boxes above.

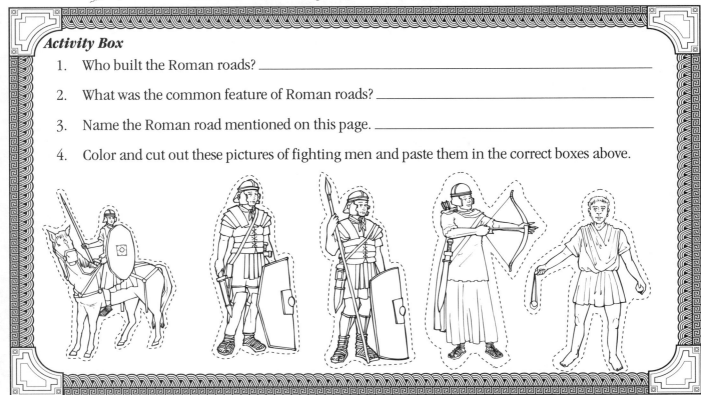

ROMAN LEGIONS – WEAPONS

The ideas for some weapons were copied from Greek technology and then the Romans made improvements. A Greek writer called Polybius wrote, "As soon as they saw Greek weapons, the Romans began to copy them. This is one of their strong points."

The Onager

This was a giant catapult used to hurl boulders or burning materials. Large boulders, as much as 50 kg in weight, could be thrown up to 500 meters. It is believed that the onager, a wild donkey, gave its name to the catapult because they both had the same rapid kicking action.

The Ballista

This was also a siege weapon which could fire arrows or metal bolts. In the first century A.D., a type of ballista was invented which would fire a succession of arrows, a similar idea to repeating weapons used in modern warfare. The ballista, in effect, was a large stationary crossbow which could fire arrows 300 meters. A weapon like the ballista can be seen on Trajan's column in Rome. It was often mounted on a cart to make it more mobile.

Siege Tower

The siege tower was built taller than the walls of the city under siege. It could be constructed out of the reach of enemy weapons and then wheeled forward, where it was very effective in breaching defensive walls.

Battering Ram (an Aries)

The wooden roof of the ram was covered with leather to protect the attackers from missiles. This weapon was used successfully by the Assyrians and Alexander the Great. It was still being used in the 1400s, when it was replaced by the siege cannon, which was more effective at breaking down walls and gates.

The Trireme

The vessel was a common warship in Mediterranean countries. The trireme had three banks of oars and was faster than the quinquereme. It was about 35 meters long and 5.5 meters wide. A metal-tipped ram at the bow pierced enemy ships at the waterline. The trireme carried crew, archers, soldiers, officers and, most of all, oarsmen. Some used grappling irons to pull ships alongside so soldiers could lower a bridge and board the enemy vessel. The trireme was also used as a trading ship to carry goods to Rome from around the Empire.

ROMAN LEGIONS – WEAPONS

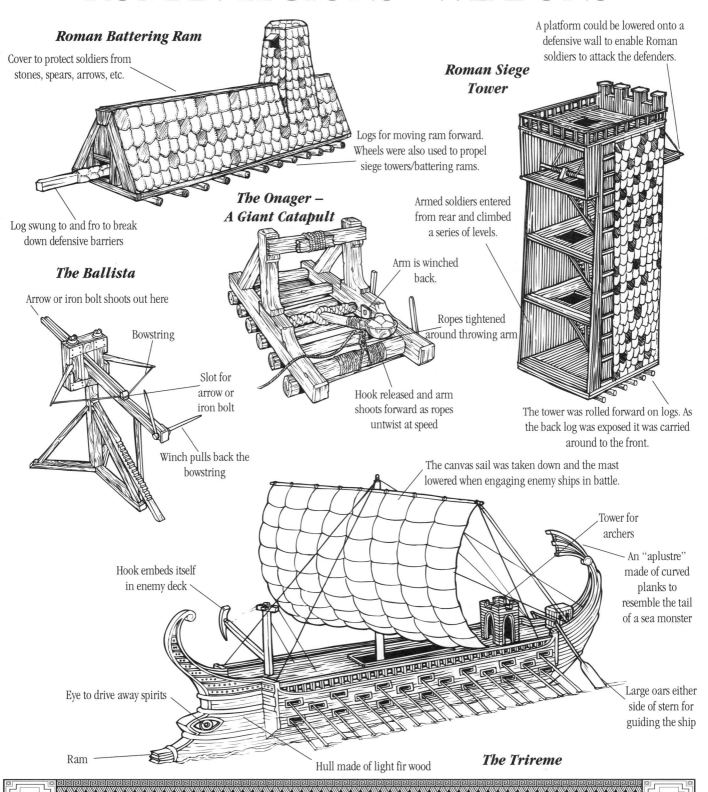

Roman Battering Ram

Cover to protect soldiers from stones, spears, arrows, etc.

Logs for moving ram forward. Wheels were also used to propel siege towers/battering rams.

Log swung to and fro to break down defensive barriers

Roman Siege Tower

A platform could be lowered onto a defensive wall to enable Roman soldiers to attack the defenders.

Armed soldiers entered from rear and climbed a series of levels.

The tower was rolled forward on logs. As the back log was exposed it was carried around to the front.

The Onager – A Giant Catapult

Arm is winched back.

Ropes tightened around throwing arm

Hook released and arm shoots forward as ropes untwist at speed

The Ballista

Arrow or iron bolt shoots out here

Bowstring

Slot for arrow or iron bolt

Winch pulls back the bowstring

The Trireme

The canvas sail was taken down and the mast lowered when engaging enemy ships in battle.

Tower for archers

An "aplustre" made of curved planks to resemble the tail of a sea monster

Hook embeds itself in enemy deck

Large oars either side of stern for guiding the ship

Eye to drive away spirits

Ram

Hull made of light fir wood

Activity Box

With a partner, use cardboard, popsicle sticks, straws and glue to make one of the Roman weapons of war shown above.

ROMAN SLAVES (1)

The Roman writer, Seneca, commenting about the harsh treatment of slaves, said, "The smallest noise is beaten back with a stick; the slaves are even beaten for letting slip a cough or a sneeze or a hiccup. If a slave killed his master as revenge for cruel treatment, all slaves in the household were executed."

It was difficult for slaves to escape as some large country estates had small prison buildings where they were locked away at night. Untrustworthy slaves worked with a chain around their ankles and one has been excavated still holding the fossilized remains of a slave's foot.

Well-educated slaves, many of them Greek, often ran businesses or shops for their masters and, if successful, could earn their freedom. Slaves granted their freedom were often rich but had no voting rights. They were called "freed" men or women, but not freemen/women, who may have been poor but had voting rights. A slave could save up money gifts (peculia) given by a master pleased with the slave's work. This money could then be used to buy his freedom at a special ceremony. By the fall of the western part of the Empire in the 5th century A.D. most slaves had achieved the status of freemen/women.

A temple on an island in the River Tiber was used to house slaves too sick or old to work, for the Emperor Claudius (A.D. 41–54) had decreed that such slaves could not be abandoned or executed. They were now free and in later years the temple became one of the world's first public hospitals.

Ancient Rome

ROMAN SLAVES (1)

It would be difficult to imagine life in Ancient Rome without slaves, for they were used in every area of daily life in the city of Rome and throughout the Empire. As their empire and the number of nations they conquered increased, the Romans had an enormous supply of cheap slave labor. Julius Caesar alone brought back over 1,000,000 captive men, women and children after the conquest of Gaul (France). Apart from prisoners of war, many criminals became slaves and were just another piece of property to be bought or sold in slave markets by their wealthy masters or by the State. Romans were often judged by the number of slaves they possessed and some rich families owned hundreds! Slaves could be given away as gifts or left to someone else when the owner died and if a female slave had children the babies were born into slavery.

A slave tag (or possibly a dog tag) unearthed by archaeologists. The translation says:
"Hold me lest I flee and return me to my master Viventius on the estate of Callistus."

Slaves worked in households as cooks and cleaners, did the hard work on farm estates and worked even harder in factories making woolen cloth or in quarries and mines around the Empire. The officials who ran Roman cities used slaves as builders' laborers, road sweepers and rubbish collectors. Strong men were often used as oarsmen on Roman warships, as charioteers in races to entertain the people, or were trained to be gladiators, as their lives were cheap. When they were too old to fight, the gladiator slaves were often thrown to the lions unless they had pleased their masters by their victories in the arena. Even in households many slaves were brutally treated, though in some homes they were treated as part of the family.

Activity Box

Write a couple of sentences about each of the following. Tell how you would feel if you were a slave and your master told you that:

(a) You were going to be trained as a gladiator to fight wild beasts in the arena.

(b) You were going to be sold to a new master who was known to be cruel.

(c) You were going to be granted your freedom as you had given excellent service.

ROMAN SLAVES (2)

Debate Notes

It is important for students to understand that passing judgement on the actions of others is especially difficult when it is in a time and culture of which we have no direct perception and understanding.

While the arguments against the proposition should be based on a human rights perspective, there is a need in debate to identify the purpose of the opposing side. As is mentioned in the notes, the Roman Empire would have had little or no chance of survival without slaves being an integral part of the community structure. Therefore, it is important to direct the students to present a strong case for both sides of the argument, as the main purpose of this activity is to gain a clearer understanding of life in these times, not to judge the Romans on their behavior.

ROMAN SLAVES (2)

As the Romans conquered nations, they used many of the people of these nations as slaves. Prepare to debate the following topic by presenting arguments for and against this proposition.

> *The ancient Romans were justified in using the people of conquered nations as slaves.*

Arguments For

1. _____
_____
_____

2. _____
_____
_____

3. _____
_____
_____

Arguments Against

1. _____
_____
_____

2. _____
_____
_____

3. _____
_____
_____

If you were to select which side you were to debate explain your choice.

_____
_____
_____

ROMAN SLAVES –
SPARTACUS

The slaves' revolt led by Spartacus frightened the citizens of Rome, for it took place in southern Italy near the seat of government and not in a province of the Empire. The Romans were keen to subdue any slave rebellions since slavery was so important to Roman daily life.

Many of the thousands who flocked to join the slave army led by Spartacus were herdsmen who were not constantly supervised like their co-workers in the crop fields and vineyards. Herdsmen weren't chained and carried weapons to defend their animals against bandits and wolves. The slave revolt wasn't a political movement to abolish slavery, it was an attempt to escape from terrible conditions and to seek revenge for the cruelties of their masters.

A general named Crassus was given six legions to crush the slaves. He was finally successful, killing some 6,000 slaves. Those who escaped were captured by another general, Pompey, who had just returned from victories in Spain.

Suggested Activity

Watch the video *Spartacus* with Kirk Douglas as the leader of the slaves. (Note: *Spartacus* is rated PG for "medium level violence" and it may be advisable to obtain parental consent.)

(a) We know from history that Spartacus appeared to be a caring leader. Give an example from the film which shows this.

(b) What did the film tell us about the Roman ruling class (patricians)?

(c) Why do you think the late Stanley Kubrick, one of Hollywood's greatest film makers, would want to make a film about Spartacus?

Note: The film shows many aspects of Roman life.

ROMAN SLAVES – SPARTACUS

Tacitus, a Roman historian, didn't think much of the Roman slaves who came from all corners of the Roman Empire. He once wrote that "fear is the only way to keep this rubbish in check," but a slave the Romans couldn't keep in check was Spartacus. He was a herdsman from Thracia, an ancient land to the northeast of Greece, and he had served in the Roman army as a member of the "auxilia," non-citizens of Rome recruited from the provinces to support the regular soldiers.

As an able-bodied slave, Spartacus was forced to become a gladiator, but in 73 B.C. he escaped from a large gladiatorial training school at Capua with about 70 slaves. In time, he was joined by vast numbers of slave farm workers and they assembled on the slopes of Mt. Vesuvius. Eventually he led an army of over 70,000 men. For many months this huge army, led by trained gladiators, ravaged large parts of southern Italy and defeated several Roman armies. Spartacus hoped his followers would later cross the Alps to seek safety in their own lands but the slaves were more interested in plundering Roman villages and towns.

Finally, after training an army of 40,000 men, politician and military leader General Crassus trapped and killed Spartacus during a battle at Apulia, only two years after the gladiators had escaped from Capua. Crassus then ordered that 6,000 of the captured slaves be killed by crucifixion.

Activity Box

1. In what year was Spartacus killed?

   _____

2. Greece lies (south, northeast, south-west, north) of Thracia.

   _____

3. Give words from the passage for:

   (a) huge _____

   (b) gathered _____

4. What were foreigners in the Roman army know as?

   _____

5. Who showed his dislike for slaves in his writings?

   _____

6. What did Spartacus want his slave army to do eventually?

   _____

7. Why do you think Crassus defeated a much bigger army?

   _____

8. Which mountains are mentioned in the passage?

   _____

9. Tacitus thought _____
   was a way of preventing slaves from rebelling.

10. Do you think it was necessary for Crassus to crucify 6,000 slaves?

    _____

    Why/Why not? _____

GOVERNMENT – THE REPUBLIC

2 consuls—the most important magistrates—elected for one year

Senate—advises the consuls. Senate made up of ex-magistrates

Assembly elects tribunes to look after the people's interests in the senate.

Magistrates elected each year. Only wealthy men took the positions as they were unpaid.

People's assembly elects the magistrates. Free Roman men can vote and the votes of the rich are worth more than those of the poor citizens.

WOMAN

NO VOTE

SLAVE

NO VOTE

Rule of the Republic by consuls and the senate lasted for nearly 500 years. Originally the senate had 100 members but this grew to 600 by the first century B.C. Senators usually held positions for life and as senators, consuls and generals came from a small group of wealthy families power was in the hands of a few, i.e., government by an oligarchy.

After their year in office, consuls could become proconsuls—governors in the provinces, the conquered countries of the Empire. Both consuls had to agree before something could be carried out so if one consul said "veto" (I forbid) the idea was dropped.

The patricians claimed that their ancestry gave them the right to rule. Even if a plebeian was as rich as a patrician, he was unable to hold a high position in the government structure. In the third century B.C., it was decided that one of the consuls should be a plebeian. Eventually the struggles for power between supporters of the senate and the people's assembly led to bloody civil war.

Purple was the color worn by people who held important positions.

The coastal waters of ancient Phoenicia contained two kinds of shellfish whose bodies contained sacs of yellowy fluid which turned purple when exposed to light. The city of Tyre was famous for the quality of its purple dye made from the shellfish. Archaeologists have found thousands of empty shells in ancient dye pits near the site of ancient Tyre. Today the shellfish are almost extinct around the coast of modern Lebanon.

Suggested Activity

Students could discuss the point that Roman women should have had the right to vote and not have been reduced to the same status as a slave.

GOVERNMENT – THE REPUBLIC

After the legendary foundation of Rome in 753 B.C., the city was ruled by kings until 509 B.C. Then the people, led by nobles, drove out the last of the Etruscan kings. A republic was then set up where power was not invested in a single king but in a group of elected people. At first there were two classes of citizens—the wealthy patricians (privileged class) who could trace their ancestry back to the first Romans and the plebeians (ordinary working people). In the early years, the plebeians had little say in the government of the Republic but they fought for equal rights. Eventually, after a series of strikes, they formed a people's assembly which excluded the patricians. This assembly elected officials called tribunes to look after their interests in the senate. At the first people's assembly, two tribunes were elected but the number was increased to ten in later years. Tribunes could speak against proposed courses of action by the magistrates of the senate if they thought those actions threatened the rights of ordinary citizens. During the Republic the senate and the people's assembly made the laws and the legal system was explained in a document called the twelve tables. The most important magistrates were the two consuls who were the heads of the government and commanders of Rome's armies.

The two consuls, who had equal powers, were guided by the senate, a body made up of ex-magistrates. In emergencies, such as invasions by barbarians, total power could be given to a dictator who held office until the crisis was over. In the later years of the Republic another class of citizens called equites (traders, bankers, businessmen) also became involved in the struggle for power.

In 27 B.C., after defeating other Roman generals in a struggle for power, General Octavian renamed himself Augustus ("revered one") and became emperor. From his rule onward this period of Roman history is known as the Empire. Like the early kings of Rome, power was again in the hands of one man for the emperor now appointed the consuls and the senators.

Roman senators wore robes with double purple stripes down the front. Purple, a dye obtained from shellfish, was the color worn by people who held important positions. Draw and color his stripes.

Activity Box

1. Which class of citizens held power? _____

2. How long did kings rule early Rome? _____

3. Which officials looked after ordinary people? _____

4. The most important magistrates were _____.

5. Whose name means "revered one"? _____

6. The twelve tables was about Roman _____.

7. The people's assembly and the _____ made laws.

8. Who held supreme power in a crisis? _____

ROMAN GODS AND GODDESSES (1)

Several emperors encouraged the worship of Mithras as the cult of Mithraism emphasized discipline, loyalty and courage. The emperors realized it was these qualities which made the Roman legions such a powerful military force. Like Christianity, followers of Mithras were promised life after death, so it was a popular cult with the Roman soldiers. Worshippers of Mithras, like Christians, believed in resurrection, baptizing to wash away sins and that their god had descended from heaven. Some historians believe that Mithraism would have become the dominant religion had Christianity not spread around the known world in those early times.

Only priests could conduct the sacrificial ceremonies, for if mistakes were made it was believed that the gods would not accept the sacrifices. Animals were examined carefully to ensure there were no blemishes on the skins or internal organs. The animals most frequently used were pigs, oxen, sheep, goats and doves. Portions of the animal were thrown onto an altar for the gods to eat.

Some historians like Livy believed that the Romans had been favored by the gods for he wrote: "Those who followed the gods had every success." After the bloody civil wars in the first century B.C., the poet Horace declared that the Romans had suffered because they had neglected their gods.

The Christians were the only religious people the Romans constantly persecuted. Christianity spread west from the Middle East and eventually the believers in only one God outnumbered the pagans, for Christianity promised the Roman citizens life after death. The Christians developed secret signs to disguise their identity from possible enemies. They would trace an outline of a fish on their palm, the Greek word for fish containing the letters of the name and title of their leader, Jesus.

ROMAN GODS AND GODDESSES (1)

Temple altar

The Romans inherited many gods and goddesses from the Greeks and some from other countries, like the Egyptian gods Isis and Serapis and the Persian god Mithras. The Etruscans introduced the Greek gods to the Romans, who adopted them but gave them Roman names, so Zeus became Jupiter and Demeter became Ceres. The Romans made animal sacrifices on altars outside the temples in order to satisfy their gods, as they believed that earthquakes, lightning and storms were signs that the gods were displeased. They thought certain gods protected groups of people like farmers, craftsmen, or the dead.

To worship their gods they built temples, each containing a statue of a particular god. Most Roman temples were rectangular in shape but a few were circular, like the Temple of Vesta where Rome's sacred flame was constantly burning.

Household shrine

Priests looked after the temples and special priests called "augurs" explained what the gods meant by signs like the shapes of clouds or flights of birds

Emperors were thought to have god-like qualities and some of the more popular ones like Augustus were worshipped as gods after they died. Wealthy citizens had shrines designed like tiny temples in their homes or gardens and worshipped their chosen gods by offering small gifts such as wine or fruit.

Each god had a feast day (or days) when celebrations were held in the streets for the Roman citizens. Prayers to the gods were private and silent and heads were covered with a toga as the citizens faced the rising sun. The Romans also believed in spirits who represented natural features like hills and rivers.

For centuries the Romans persecuted the Christians, who believed in only one God. The Christians were blamed for the great fire which destroyed parts of Rome and, as they refused to bow down to statues of Roman gods, hundreds were arrested, burned to death, or thrown to the lions in the public arena. To escape their persecutors or to worship in secret, the Christians would often hide in tunnels called catacombs, which spread for hundreds of kilometers beneath the city of Rome.

---

1. Underline the key words in the passage above.

2. Use these words to complete this myth about Ceres, goddess of agriculture.

mother	angry	return	fertile	Saturn	journey	agriculture
barren	third	taught	seeds	took	search	persuaded
eating	flowers	delighted	carried	ailing	underworld	

Ceres was the daughter of the god _____ [1]. While her own daughter was gathering

_____ [2] she was seized and _____ [3] off by the god Pluto to his _____ [4] of

the dead. Ceres was very _____ [5] and made the earth _____ [6] before setting off to

_____ [7] for her daughter, Proserpina. On her _____ [8] she saved the _____ [9]

son of King Celeus. Ceres _____ [10] the boy away with her and _____ [11] him all about

_____ [12]. The gods _____ [13] Pluto to return Proserpina to her _____ [14]

but he tricked her into _____ [15] some special pomegranate _____ [16] so she had to

spend one _____ [17] of the year in Hades. Ceres was _____ [18] about her daughter's

_____ [19] and made the earth _____ [20] again.

ROMAN GODS AND GODDESSES (2)

Jupiter

He was the most powerful god, protector of Rome and ruler of the universe. Jupiter was a sky god of thunder and lightning whose symbols were the eagle and the thunderbolt. Ancient astronomers named a planet after Jupiter, who was the son of Saturn. His temple was the religious center of Rome and his temples were built in every Roman town. When the consuls were appointed in January each year, bulls were sacrificed to thank Jupiter for his protection the previous year.

Mars

Mars was the god of war and Romans prayed to him for successes over their enemies. He was especially important as he was thought to be the father of Romulus and Remus. Originally the god of farmland, March is named after him as it was the start of the Roman growing season. The planet Mars was named after him because of its angry red color. When war broke out a Roman consul had to shake the god's sacred spears and cry "Mars vigila" — "Mars, wake up!"

Neptune

God of the sea and son of Saturn, Neptune was said to be half man and half fish. Statues show him with a trident, a three-pronged spear, which he used to raise or quiet storms at sea. Sailors prayed to him for a safe journey and the world famous Trevi Fountain in Rome includes a statue of Neptune, who also had a planet named after him.

Minerva

As the daughter of Jupiter, she was an important goddess. She was the goddess of arts and crafts and education and her temple was a popular meeting place for artists, actors and poets. Her main festival was in March and later she became the goddess of wisdom and war.

Mercury

Jupiter's messenger and god of roads and travel. He wore winged sandals and was also the god of trade. His name has given us the words "merchant" and "commerce." He was the son of Jupiter and snakes wound around his staff protected him on his travels. His first temple was built in 495 B.C. and his name has also been given to a planet.

(continued on page 40)

Ancient Rome

ROMAN GODS AND GODDESSES (2)

Jupiter		Neptune	
Minerva		**Mercury**	
Ceres		**Mars**	
Bacchus		**Janus**	

Activity Box

Listen to or read the information provided by the teacher. Then write words in the boxes to describe each god/goddess.

ROMAN GODS AND GODDESSES (3)

Ceres

An Earth goddess of agriculture, especially fruit and grain—"cereal" comes from her name. She was worshipped by farmers and the common people of Rome. Her temple built in 493 B.C. was damaged by fire in 31 B.C., but rebuilt by the Emperor Augustus Caesar.

Janus

The two-headed god, with one face looking to the future and the other looking at the historical past. This god guarded doors and archways and gave us the name of our first month as he was seen as the protector of the start of life. His festival day was January 9 and his worship dates back to Rome's early years. In 235 B.C., the doors of the temple of Janus were closed to show Rome was at peace with all nations for the first time.

Bacchus

The festivals for Bacchus, the Roman god of wine, were drinking feasts which were originally held in secret and attended by women only. Their reputation for drunkenness and riots resulted in the senate passing a decree to ban them except for special occasions. The Romans began to worship Bacchus after coming into contact with Greek customs around 700 B.C.

ROMAN GODS AND GODDESSES (3)

Jupiter	**Neptune**
Minerva	**Mercury**
Ceres	**Mars**
Bacchus	**Janus**

Activity Box

Listen to or read the information provided by the teacher. Create a symbol that could be used to represent each god/goddess, based on what you know about each one.

Ancient Rome

ROMAN LIFE–HOMES (1)

A survey in Rome in A.D. 350 indicated that the number of apartment blocks was over 45,000. These "insulae" had no internal drains, so waste was often thrown into the street gutters, as the early Romans were unaware of the connection between health and poor hygiene.

After the Romans defeated the Greek settlements of southern Italy around 250 B.C., they adopted their grid system of city streets built at right angles to each other. They then added Roman features—the forum, the center of Roman cities where government and religious buildings were found, the amphitheater for public entertainment, the public baths and water systems.

Fire was a constant risk in Rome's wooden buildings so the emperor, Augustus, set up fire brigades, each with 1,000 firemen, to cover different areas throughout the city. They used simple hand pumps and wet sponges to dampen wooden walls to prevent a fire from spreading.

Most surviving Roman furniture is made of metal or marble because the more common wooden furniture has rotted over the centuries. As rich Romans often ate outside in their pleasant climate, tables were commonly made of marble or some other stone.

The wicks in the oil lamps were made from the stems of plants which were dipped into wax and then twisted together into a kind of rope similar to tapers today. Thousands of Roman lamps have survived because they were made of metal or fired clay. Lanterns were also widely used, with the flame being protected by pieces of horn or an animal bladder.

ROMAN LIFE-HOMES (1)

The homes of the shepherds in Rome's earliest days were merely one-roomed huts with a hole in the roof to let out smoke from a fire. As Rome expanded over the centuries, land was scarce, so builders had to build upwards. By the third century A.D., most people lived in an insula, a block of apartments similar to our modern apartment buildings. Poor people couldn't afford houses so they rented a small room in an insula, even though rent for apartments owned by the upper classes (patricians) was often quite high. Builders could normally build up to five or six stories and some apartments

on the lower levels were quite luxurious and spacious. Poor tenants lived in the upper stories, which were usually built of wood, not stone like those below. Not many insulae had their own toilets, so tenants had to use public latrines. Sponges, used instead of toilet tissue, were washed clean in the constant flow of water along a narrow channel in front of the seats.

Roman homes didn't have electricity and were lit by oil lamps or wax candles. Oil lamps, also used to illuminate streets, burned vegetable oil from olives, nuts or sesame seeds, or fish oil. With southern Italy's mild winters, heating wasn't a big problem. Open fires in metal braziers, using wood or coal but mainly charcoal for fuel, were found in many homes. Braziers in the wooden sections of insulae could have been a fire hazard, especially if used for cooking meals in the hot, dry summers. There was no running water so it was carried from public fountains by family slaves.

The villas of the rich, usually country houses attached to farms, were luxurious and sometimes contained 20 or 30 rooms. They had private baths, mosaic patterns on the floor and some even had glass windows in the upper rooms. Villas usually contained a central atrium, with a glass skylight, where guests were welcomed to the household.

Furniture such as tables, chairs, couches, or cupboards was only used in the larger rooms like the atrium. Unlike the simply-made furniture of the poor, villas contained elegant tables, beds and chairs often inlaid with ivory, shells, marble and decorative woods. Early mirrors were bronze or silver, highly polished, but by the fifth century A.D. they were made of glass.

Open metal brazier

ROMAN LIFE – HOMES (2)

The hypocaust system for heating houses was invented in 85 B.C. and developed in the first century A.D. In Italy's warm climate it was mainly used in the public baths, but in the colder regions of the Empire like Britain and mainland Europe it was often used in town houses and country villas.

The warm air circulated under the floors and inside the walls. Once the bricks or concrete were heated they retained their warmth for a long time.

Because the furnace constantly required wood, the hypocaust was expensive to run. The temperature was not easily controlled; this was probably done by adding more fuel or reducing the supply. In public baths, the hot air was directed to the hottest rooms first and then, as the air cooled, on to the cooler rooms. A boiler over the furnace provided hot water. Baked bricks were used to support the floors above the hypocaust and sometimes to line the ducts carrying the hot air.

"The simple life of the poor involves suffering every day—a pot with a broken handle, a fireplace without fire, a beggar's rug, an old camp bed riddled with bed bugs …"

Martial
First Century AD

Martial was a poet who was born in Spain but lived in Rome for many years. He described many characters from everyday life in his poems.

Activity Suggestion

1. The class could discuss/write opinions on the statement "It is better to be poor today than in Roman times." (Answers could include the help given to the poor today, e.g., no income tax, welfare groups like the Salvation Army, assisted State housing/rents.)

2. Using clay or Plasticine make a simple Roman oil lamp. Use vegetable oil and a rope or string wick. Allow the wick to soak up the oil before it is lit by an adult.

ROMAN LIFE – HOMES (2)

Hypocaust system

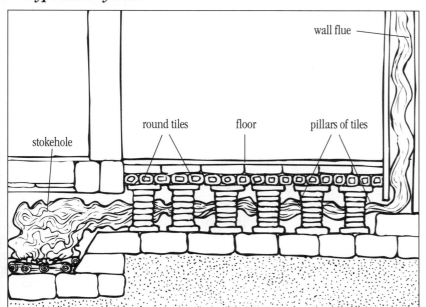

wall flue

round tiles

floor

pillars of tiles

stokehole

The Romans had central heating systems called "hypocausts." They were mainly found in the colder parts of the Roman Empire. A network of channels using bricks, tiles, or concrete was constructed under a house, usually the villa of a wealthy Roman. A furnace was continually fed with wood by a household slave. The warm air circulated under the floor and passed along ducts in the walls before escaping under the eaves. Granaries in Roman provinces in the colder and damper parts of northern Europe were long buildings in which grain was stored. The grain was spread out on the floor and the hypocaust system underneath dried it out before it was stored for future use.

Activity Box

Read your notes on Roman life in their homes and answer these questions.

1. Why did thousands of poor Romans live in insulae?

   _____

2. Why were hypocausts used in northern Europe?

   _____

3. Who was responsible for bringing water to the household?

   _____

4. What did the Romans have for street lighting?

   _____

5. What kind of patterns were found on the floors of wealthy homes?

   _____

6. In which room were guests welcomed to the house?

   _____

7. What did shepherds live in during the earliest days of Rome?

   _____

8. Why did Roman builders have to build upwards?

   _____

9. Which word means a kind of open stove?

   _____

10. Why do you think glass windows were usually only used in upper rooms?

    _____

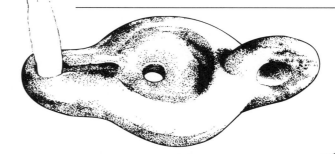

ROMAN LIFE – HOMES (3)

Thousands of mosaics have been found in excavated buildings. Usually, the styles of the designs help to date them. Mosaics were mainly used on floors or walls but sometimes on ceilings from the first century A.D. They were used throughout the Empire for ornate decoration in both public and private buildings. Much later, expensive materials like gold and glass were used on the walls and ceilings of church buildings. Some mosaics were designed as maps, giving geographical information on various regions of the Roman Empire.

Mosaics are valuable sources of information for experts studying life in Roman times. Mosaic panels of scenes from around the Empire show pictures of their gods, groups of hippopotamus hunters, picnic parties under the trees, flying ibises, farming scenes, pleasure barges, temple scenes with robed priests and worshippers—the whole range of life at that time.

If the pattern or scene was a complicated one, the pieces of stone had to be much smaller to capture the finer details of the picture. Sometimes, over a million tiny cubes of stone would be used in a mosaic which might only be one square meter in area.

Note: For Activity 1, discontinued tiles can be obtained free or inexpensively from tile retailers.

ROMAN LIFE – HOMES (3)

A mosaic found at Herculaneum

M osaics on the floors or walls of Roman villas were patterns or pictures made up of thousands of tiny, colored cubes of stone called "tesserae."

They were pressed into wet plaster or concrete to form scenes, geometric patterns, or portraits. Roman mosaics developed from Greek mosaics around the second century B.C. Most used colored stones or tiles, but some were just black and white. There were mosaicists who designed patterns and cut the stones into the required shapes before they were delivered to a site.

Activity Box

1. Follow the procedure for the pattern or the picture to make your own mosaic.

    pattern

    picture

    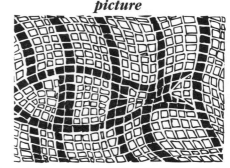

    A mosaic of sea creatures was found in Pompeii's ruins.

    (a) Use centimeter-square graph paper and cut off a rectangle 8 cm x 10 cm.

    (b) Draw centimeter squares on colored card. Use three different colors. You could share colors if working in a group of three.

    (c) Cut up the colored card into centimeter squares.

    (d) Decide on a pattern and glue the colored squares onto the rectangle.

    (e) You could cut your colored squares along a diagonal and use the resulting triangles in your design.

    (f) Your finished artwork should give you the effect of a Roman mosaic.

    (a) Get an adult/teacher to break up colored ceramic tiles/plates inside a couple of strong plastic bags using a hammer.

    (b) Use the shallow lid of an old plastic lunch box or cardboard box to make a frame.

    (c) Spread soft modeling clay over the lid/ frame or mix some cement/plaster of Paris into a thick consistency (one part cement, three parts sand and one part water).

    (d) Partly press broken crockery/tiles into the plaster/cement and design a pattern or picture of your own.

2. Describe your artwork. _____

    _____

3. Describe any difficulties and how you overcame them. _____

    _____

ROMAN LIFE – FOOD (1)

Evidence for the kinds of food eaten by the Romans is provided by the writers of those times, by archaeological excavations which have uncovered nuts, grain seeds and animal bones, and by thousands of wall paintings and mosaics.

The poor could buy grain cheaply at first but in the first century B.C., it was provided free for thousands of families. During the later years, in the reign of the Emperor Augustus, about one-third of Rome's population of 300,000 were being fed by the government. Eventually, when the government was providing free cooking oil, pork fat and sometimes wine, the financial burden was too heavy and the system was discontinued.

Circular, domed ovens were mainly used to bake bread or pastries. The embers were raked out before the uncooked bread was placed inside. Country people generally made tough black bread. Townspeople who could afford it bought softer white bread from the bakeries.

Most food in the wealthier households was cooked over a charcoal-filled brazier or on a hearth with containers suspended over the flames. Any smoke escaped through the roof or wall vents.

As the Empire spread eastwards, new spices and different ways of cooking foods were introduced to Rome.

ROMAN LIFE – FOOD (1)

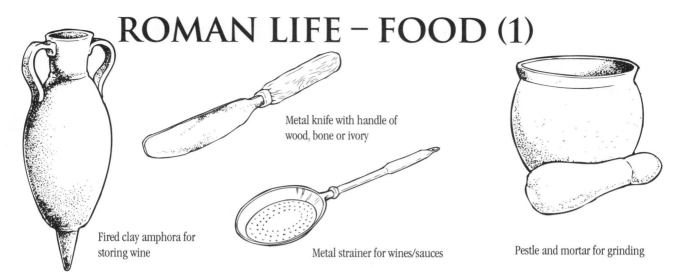

Fired clay amphora for storing wine

Metal knife with handle of wood, bone or ivory

Metal strainer for wines/sauces

Pestle and mortar for grinding

The poor citizens of Rome had a basic diet, mainly a kind of porridge made from wheat boiled in water, which they ate from simple earthenware bowls. Eventually, when the Romans discovered how to make bread, the grain porridge became less popular. In addition, cheese from goat's milk, eggs, onions, olives and a variety of vegetables were eaten. The poor couldn't afford to eat meat regularly but were sometimes provided with some after animal sacrifices. They couldn't cook meals in the confined spaces in their small homes because of the risk of fire. Hot meals were generally purchased from food shops, such as bakeries, located on the ground floors of apartment blocks, or eaten in local taverns.

To keep the poor citizens contented and prevent revolts, they were often given free food ("annona") and entertainment. However, in the later years of the Empire the growing population meant the government could no longer afford the expense.

Wealthy Romans used sauces, herbs like oregano and thyme, and spices like nutmeg or ginger on their foods. Meat from chickens, pigs, wild boars and deer was also popular. Meals also included fish and shellfish, for there were many coastal fishing boats supplying shops and families, and fish in the rivers and seas were plentiful.

Fresh fruit and a variety of cakes made from corn and sweetened with honey often completed the meal, along with wine from local and overseas vineyards.

While poor Romans couldn't afford a kitchen, in most rich households the kitchen was quite spacious and well equipped. A wood fire was generally used for cooking and food was grilled or sometimes boiled in bronze containers placed on metal stands over the fire. Kitchen slaves were able to use sharp knives, spits for roasting meat over the fire and pottery vessels ("amphorae") to hold wine and cooking oils.

ROMAN LIFE – FOOD (2)

See page 45 for Roman Life — Food background information and teacher's notes.

Additional Activities

Compare food in Roman times with food in the families of your community. Consider:

(a)   how the food is obtained.

(b)   how the food is prepared/cooked.

(c)   type of food.

(d)   differences in diets between the rich and the poor.

(e)   how food is packaged.

(f)   how food is stored.

(g)   variety of food available.

ROMAN LIFE – FOOD (2)

Food in Roman times was definitely at two levels, one for the poor and one for the rich. Use the information contained in the text to prepare a daily menu for a poor family and a rich family.

Poor Family	*Wealthy Family*
Morning Meal	Morning Meal
Midday Meal	Midday Meal
Evening Meal	Evening Meal

Describe below how each of the families would obtain/cook their food.

Poor Family

_____

_____

_____

_____

_____

Wealthy Family

_____

_____

_____

_____

_____

ROMAN LIFE – FOOD (3)

The great vineyards of France were first planted by the Roman occupation forces.

Wine was often diluted with water as drinking pure wine was thought to be barbaric. It was also added to water to purify it, used as an antiseptic on wounds and used to preserve food. Though they used honey, the Romans didn't have sugar, so sweet wine was a valued part of their diet.

Poor people drank low-quality wine called "acetum." They had milk but it was thought to be an uncivilized drink, fit only for making cheese or for medicinal purposes.

Storing wine was a problem until corks were used in the later years of the Empire. Lead or wax was used to seal the wine storage jars but often air leaked in and the wine became vinegary. Though cider and beer were drunk in parts of the Empire, wine was the popular drink in Rome. It was so popular that Roman writer Marcus Cato even suggested that working slaves on farms should be issued with it.

Meals in rich households included shellfish, edible snails, fish, roasted duck, or chicken, game birds like pheasants, dormice cooked in honey and even parrots and ostriches from North Africa. Pork, ham and venison were also popular. Olives, grapes, apricots, figs, dates, cherries and plums were just some of a huge range of fruits. An excavated rubbish dump near Rome revealed how important olives were to the Romans — it contained around forty million pots used for carrying olive oil.

Both freshwater and saltwater fish were served, with many different recipes for mullet, mackerel and tuna. Fish were cooked in spicy sauces and oysters were a delicacy.

As there were no refrigerators, the Romans had problems keeping fish or meat fresh. Ice cubes were used but only the wealthy could afford the complicated systems required.

In the days of the Republic, only men could attend formal dinners arranged to entertain guests but in later imperial times, the years when emperors ruled, women often dined with men on such occasions.

Activity Suggestion

Follow the steps in this procedure and make this dessert of stuffed dates eaten by wealthy Romans.

1. Mix together chopped-up apple and crushed nuts with breadcrumbs or cake crumbs.

2. Add small amounts of cinnamon or nutmeg.

3. Add a small quantity of fruit juice and mash into a paste.

4. Cut off the top of the dates and take out the stones.

5. Push in the mashed filling with a knife or spoon. Enjoy your meal!

ROMAN LIFE – FOOD (3)

The Romans did not have tea or coffee. They learned how to grow vines and make wine from the Greeks. They drank wine frequently, for their water supplies were often impure. Grapes for wine were grown in the Republic but also imported from France, Spain, Portugal and other regions of the Empire. The wine was usually transported in amphorae—large pottery jars. Sometimes these jars were partly buried in the ground to keep the wine cool.

The rich enjoyed entertaining guests by presenting acrobats, poets and jugglers at household feasts. Sometimes, talented slaves were used to entertain the diners, who lounged on comfortable couches as they ate. Any food scraps were thrown onto the floor for slaves to clean up. The Romans ate with their fingers. Forks were unknown and knives and spoons were usually used only in the kitchen,

The Romans crushed grapes by treading them or using a grape press.

though spoons were used with soups and other liquid dishes. Slaves served the food and washed the fingers of the guests between courses. The main meal of the day was in the evening after the visit to the public baths. It included meat, seafood, vegetables, honey cakes and fruit.

Activity Box

Color the diagrams of foods eaten in wealthy households. Then write them in alphabetical order in the second set of boxes.

Grapes	Dates	Mushrooms	Porridge
Pork	Bread	Nuts	Vegetables
Venison	Honey	Olives	Chicken
Eggs	Prawns	Fish	Cheese

ROMAN LIFE – EDUCATION

As imported Egyptian papyrus paper made from water plant fibers was expensive, pupils carved their work on wax tablets with a stylus. This writing tool had a pointed end for carving numbers or letters. The other end was flat to scrape away errors or work no longer required. As the Romans didn't know about paper made from wood pulp, the teachers had books made from papyrus, but also used "vellum" made from the hides of cattle, sheep and goats. When papyrus sheets were glued together in book form they were known as "volumen," from which our word "volume" is derived. Quill pens were used to write with, ink being made from soot, gum and sepia, the ink-like fluid secreted by cuttlefish.

The Latin word for books is "liber" (meaning bark). Recent evidence suggests that thin sheets of wood were the most common writing material in northern parts of the Empire where papyrus wasn't easily obtained. Evidence has also been unearthed of writing scratched on pottery fragments with a stylus.

The word abacus is derived from "abax," an ancient Greek word believed to have come from an older Semitic word meaning "dust." The first abacus was a tray filled with sand (or dust) and trading calculations were drawn in the sand and then wiped out. Early Roman abacuses were just lines on a marble top with small, movable discs for recording calculations. On later Roman types, the discs were moved up and down in grooves on a metal or stone surface. Actual examples of Roman abacuses have been found in excavations.

One Greek pedagogue called Livius Andronicus translated Homer's famous poem "The Odyssey" into Latin, the Roman language, so his students could read it. This was the first piece of Greek literature translated into Latin.

Discipline in schools was severe but Quintilian, a writer and leading rhetor (teacher of public speaking), disapproved of corporal punishment and wrote about the need for high personal standards for teachers.

Around midday, schoolchildren joined the rest of the Roman population (mainly the rich) in a siesta, when people rested or slept to avoid the midday heat.

ROMAN LIFE – EDUCATION

Reed pen used with ink.

Stylus used on wax.

In the early years of the Republic, boys were taught to read, write and how to handle weapons by their fathers. An educational system developed from the third century B.C. with educated Greek slaves (pedagogues) or freedmen as teachers. Girls did not attend schools for many were legally married at 12. Their mothers trained them at home to read and write and how to run a household, though girls in some rich families were taught by pedagogues. Girls began to attend schools in the later years of the Republic. After the reign of the emperor Augustus, the position of women in Rome's society improved and some became teachers. The sons of wealthy families were taught in schools or by private tutors. Many poor children, who could also be slaves, had little chance of an education, for they worked long hours.

Children first attended primary school from the age of six or seven. The lessons were basic, with an emphasis on writing, reading and learning to count on an abacus. The alphabet was learned letter by letter and sometimes sweets were shaped into letters, perhaps as a reward when a letter was learned!

Wax tablets held together with leather thonging to form a type of book which could have several pages.

At the age of 12, students were taught by a grammaticus, a man with a wider knowledge than previous teachers. Students now studied poetry, history, geography and grammar. At 16, promising students from good families studied public speaking with rhetors. Such studies were essential if a young man aspired to an important position in Roman society. They were also sent to famous educational centers like Athens, where they were taught by great philosophers such as Socrates and Aristotle. The Romans admired Greek culture so the Greek language was studied by older students, who could then read books by great Greek writers like Homer.

Schools started early, often before sunrise, and finished in the early afternoon to avoid the fierce heat of the day. The cane was commonly used for disobedience, but also for students who did not learn their work quickly.

Comprehension

1. Why do you think fathers taught their sons how to handle weapons? _____

   _____

2. Which instrument was used for counting? _____

3. Why did schools start and finish early? _____

4. If a young man wanted an important position, what did he need to study? _____

   _____

5. Do you think girls should have been able to attend school in the early Republic? _____

   Why/Why not? _____

   _____

Activity Box

Follow the steps in this procedure to make a wax writing tablet used by Roman school students.

1. Find a shallow lid from a small box.

2. Use soft modeling clay or melted candle wax to fill up the lid.

3. Use the point of a compass to carve out a simple message to a partner.

4. Then, as the Roman writer, Ovid, advised, "Whenever you write, make sure all previous letters have been erased from your tablet."

ROMAN LIFE – PUBLIC BATHS

Hot air or steam baths were in use in Greece in the fifth century B.C. and gradually spread to Rome. During the Imperial years, Roman emperors built bathhouses, which became bigger and more opulent as the years passed. Rich citizens would often pay the bath fees of the poor in return for their votes.

Steam and hot water were provided from boilers made of lead or copper like those found in excavations at Pompeii. The boilers were situated above the furnaces in the hypocaust system and were supported by large iron beams.

Bathhouses were usually built around a line of symmetry, with important rooms around the center and less important areas round the outside. For many years, mixed bathing was allowed in public baths, but many bathers were often drunk after imbibing too much wine and their scandalous behavior was criticized frequently. Mixed bathing was eventually banned by the Roman Emperor Hadrian. Roman writer and philosopher, Lucius Seneca, wrote about the incessant noise from drunken bathers, food and drink sellers, and the pained yells of bathers having the hair under their armpits pulled out by hair-pluckers!

ROMAN LIFE – PUBLIC BATHS

Using a strigil.

The Roman standards of hygiene were far higher than other nations of that time, but public baths in Rome provided much more than washing facilities to satisfy the Roman concern for cleanliness. At first, public baths were small rooms with slaves filling and emptying the water by hand, but the invention of the hypocaust heating system enabled much bigger rooms to be built. Aqueducts delivered millions of liters of water and sewers built of stone or occasionally wood were built under the streets to carry away overflow water and waste from the baths and their public toilets. Rich Romans often had private baths in their homes, but in later years both poor and rich citizens could be seen at the public baths, which had become very popular as meeting places. By the second century A.D., Rome had over 1,000 public baths where hot water was cheap or free to the poor, who were given financial aid by the State.

The most appealing were the "Thermae." These contained a recreation room where bathers would exercise or loosen up with a ball game. They would then undress and perspire in a hot room where sometimes the floor was so hot because of the

hypocaust system they wore wooden clogs called "patterns." Then the bathers would clean their skin with oil, or soap made from animal fats, as soap which lathered was still unknown. Bone, bronze, or iron instruments called "strigils" were then used to scrape the oil, sweat and dead skin from the body. Rich men usually had slaves to perform this task. A hot bath followed, before taking a final plunge into a large cold bath. The outside walls of many thermae were often plain and devoid of any decoration, but inside were marble columns, vaulted ceilings, fountains, mosaic floors and fine, sculptured statues. They also contained bars, wine shops, cafes, gardens, rest rooms and even libraries and theaters.

Activity Box

List the similarities and differences between modern swimming pool/fitness centers and the public baths of ancient Rome.

Similarities	Differences
Both have cafes	The Romans sold wine
1.	1.
2.	2.
3.	3.
4.	4.
5.	5.

ROMAN LIFE – ENTERTAINMENT (1)

Amphitheaters

Originally, public games were held as part of some religious festivals, but eventually entertainment for the citizens became important in itself, and by 100 B.C. games were held throughout the year. Military leaders also began to celebrate their victories by organizing spectacular private games. Games celebrating Emperor Trajan's victory over the Dacians lasted over three months and over 11,000 animals died during the spectacle. So many animals were imported for the contests that leopards, lions and rhinoceroses were wiped out in the North African regions of the Empire. A few days before the games, copies of the program were nailed on trees or other prominent places.

Whereas theaters were Greek in origin, amphitheaters were Roman and mostly found in the western regions of the Empire. The first known amphitheater was found in Pompeii and dates back to the first century B.C. The Colosseum in Rome was begun by Emperor Vespasian and completed in 80 A.D. by his son, the Emperor Titus. Though there is little archaeological evidence, it is believed that some amphitheaters were flooded in order to hold mock sea battles between gladiators in small ships. The Colosseum had around 80 numbered entrances to help spectators to find their seats easily. Huge canvas awnings protected spectators from sun and rain. Below the arena were the cells which held gladiators, animals and prisoners. The word "arena" literally means "sand," which was strewn around the ground to soak up blood from the contests.

The training schools for gladiators were taken over by the State in the first century A.D. as it was feared they could become private armies of trained fighters and a possible threat to the State. Gladiatorial contests were eventually banned by the Emperor Honorius (395–423 A.D.) but modern bullfights like those in Spain, once a region of the Empire, are a reminder of the ancient Roman games.

At Caerleon, in Wales, are the remains of the only fully excavated Roman amphitheater in existence in Britain. Caerleon was built by an Augustan legion and was one of the largest military sites in Europe.

In the year 2000, the ancient Greek tragedy *Oedipus Rex* was performed in the Colosseum by the Greek National Theater, the first spectacle staged there in over 1,400 years. With private donations and millions of dollars a week from a special lottery, renovations are being carried out on the Colosseum and other important ancient Roman ruins.

Film companies and other commercial operators have been kept out of the Colosseum to prevent unnecessary damage. The depiction of the arena in the film *Gladiator* was done by digital imagery.

ROMAN LIFE – ENTERTAINMENT (1)

Public entertainment in the amphitheaters, circuses and theaters was an important part of life in Rome. Juvenal, a Roman writer who often criticized Roman society, wrote that ordinary citizens were only interested in "bread and circuses." Ruling magistrates and emperors used the games in the amphitheaters as a means of gaining votes during elections and also to keep the Roman population under control. The spectacular games cost enormous sums of money but admission was free.

A retiarius

A bestiarius (fought animals)

A murmillo

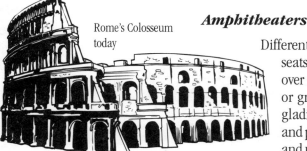

Rome's Colosseum today

Amphitheaters

Different kinds of shows were presented in these huge structures with rows of seats overlooking an arena. Rome's Colosseum is believed to have held over 50,000 spectators, who watched bloodshed for amusement as gladiators or groups of slaves fought to the death. Many gladiators were trained in gladiatorial schools and included slaves, criminals condemned to death and prisoners of war. Sometimes, trained women slaves fought in the arena and unarmed Christians were forced to face wild animals. A losing gladiator was judged by the spectators. If he had fought well he received the "thumbs up" sign, but a "thumbs down" sign meant death. Successful gladiators were crowd favorites and could become rich or win freedom from slavery. The gladiators fought wild animals on foot or occasionally from horseback. At first, fights with wild beasts took place in the mornings and public executions at noon, while fights between gladiators were held in the afternoons. Over the years, these arrangements changed.

Activity Box

1. Who criticized the Roman citizens?

   _____

2. Why did emperors pay for the games?

   _____

3. Which gladiators could become rich?

   _____

4. When were public executions?

   _____

5. What did a bestiarius fight?

   _____

6. Where were gladiators trained?

   _____

7. Give your own definition of "freedom."

   _____

8. The area where gladiators fought was the

   _____.

9. Which gladiator used a three-pronged spear?

   _____

10. Who faced animals without weapons?

    _____

11. List three things you don't like about the Roman forms of public entertainment.

    (a) _____

    (b) _____

    (c) _____

ROMAN LIFE – ENTERTAINMENT (2)

Circuses (The word "circus" comes from the Greek word "kirkos" meaning a circle—perhaps the shape of a race track.)

A chariot called a "biga" was pulled by two horses, and one pulled by four horses was a "quadriga." (Point out the Latin prefixes "bi" and "quad.") The chariots had spoked wheels and were beautifully decorated. A chariot which lost its rider could still be declared the winner if it crossed the winning line first. Chariot racing was very expensive, so it was run as a profitable business. Though chariot races were fast and required skill, the Romans didn't use chariots in battle. Like modern sporting teams, there was great rivalry among the supporters of the four chariot teams, which sometimes led to violence. At one circus in the eastern part of the Empire, thousands were killed when supporters rioted. Charioteers wore leather protective clothing in case their chariots overturned. Many drivers were slaves and some could earn sufficient money to buy their freedom if they were successful.

Circus buildings were similar in construction to the Greek hippodromes, but archaeologists are not certain that the Roman circuses were developed from the Greek structures. Though athletes sometimes raced in circuses where a town had no stadium, Roman stadiums were purpose-built to hold athletics meetings and wrestling.

Consus, a god of granaries, had an underground altar in the Circus Maximus which was uncovered during the god's festivals in August and December. During the April festival for Ceres, the goddess of agriculture, foxes with burning branches tied to their tails were let loose in the Circus Maximus—so it appears these predators were as much trouble to farmers in Ancient Rome as they are today!

"If it were the speed of the horses or the skill of the drivers that attracted the spectators, there would be some point to it. But it's only the colors worn by the drivers they go to see."

Roman nobleman's comments on the circus races.

ROMAN LIFE – ENTERTAINMENT (2)

Circuses

Roman circuses were racetracks used for chariot races, which were popular with thousands of Roman citizens. The Romans packed into the circus to cheer on their teams—the blues, greens, reds and whites—who wore tunics dyed with their team color like the rest of their clothing. Chariot racing was the oldest and most popular entertainment in the Roman world and huge amounts of money were gambled on the teams and favorite charioteers. So much money was gambled at circus races, some emperors set limits on how much could be spent.

Pick a team color and color in your charioteer and the decoration on the horses' heads.

A biga chariot

Perhaps it was popular because men and women could sit together, whereas in amphitheaters women sat at the back. The earliest circus in Rome was the giant Circus Maximus which could seat over 150,000 spectators and hold up to 250,000. Unfortunately, the building has not survived. A race could include up to 12 chariots which went around seven laps and covered about eight kilometers. As each lap was completed, a marker was taken down so the charioteers would know how far

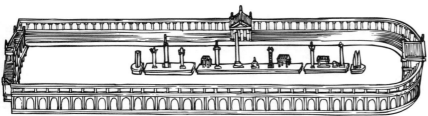

The Circus Maximus

they had raced. The chariots were very light for maximum speed and serious injuries, even deaths, were common. Successful charioteers became famous and as popular as Formula 1 drivers today.

Circuses were also used for occasional horse races, athletics and contests between gladiators.

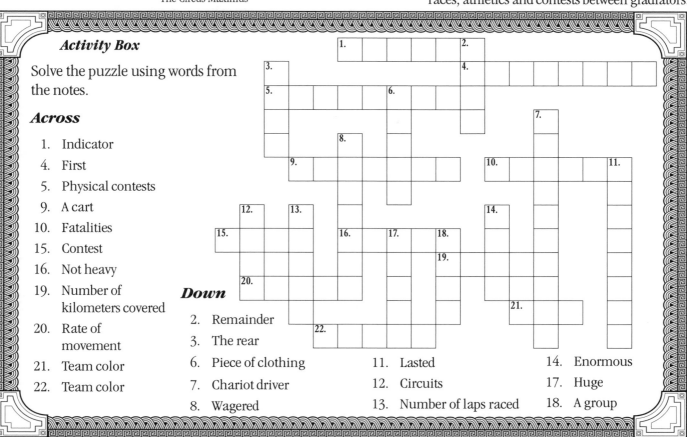

Activity Box

Solve the puzzle using words from the notes.

Across

1. Indicator
4. First
5. Physical contests
9. A cart
10. Fatalities
15. Contest
16. Not heavy
19. Number of kilometers covered
20. Rate of movement
21. Team color
22. Team color

Down

2. Remainder
3. The rear
6. Piece of clothing
7. Chariot driver
8. Wagered
11. Lasted
12. Circuits
13. Number of laps raced
14. Enormous
17. Huge
18. A group

ROMAN LIFE – ENTERTAINMENT (3)

Theaters

Roman actors were mainly men because women were only allowed to act in pantomimes and mimes. Women in the audience were also discriminated against for they weren't permitted to sit near the front. It was believed that they would run off with one of the actors if given the opportunity!

From 300 B.C., the theaters in Rome were simple, temporary wooden buildings in the forum, a market square surrounded by public buildings, or in the Circus Maximus. It wasn't until the first century B.C., during the time of Julius Caesar, that the first stone theater was built. For support, the Greeks often built their theaters into the hillsides, which meant the banks of seats overlooking the stage were easier to construct. However, most permanent Roman theaters were freestanding buildings of stone with curved tiers of seats for the audience.

The orchestra, the flat space between the stage and the audience, was reserved for senators, priests and other important officials. The audience was sheltered from sun and rain by a canvas awning. A curtain at the back of the stage hid the scene changes. The members of the audience were controlled and lectured if they were noisy and mothers were not allowed to bring their babies.

An official, an aedile, would hire actors for a play and hold rehearsals in his own home. Before the performance an actor read out the prologue, an introduction to the play, giving details of plot and characters.

Theater masks appear a lot in Roman art on wall frescoes and in mosaics. They were probably made of stiffened material such as linen.

Activity Suggestion

Students could use their masks and make up a play (in groups) to perform for the class. Remind the groups that the Romans liked comedies with songs and music.

Ancient Rome

ROMAN LIFE – ENTERTAINMENT (3)

Theaters

1. Use the words below to complete the passage.

masks	slaves	horns	earlier	origins	speaking	entertain	presented	talk
poets	mouth	heroes	afford	enjoyed	wealthier	characters	instruments	
actor	music	actors	comedy	women	audiences	legendary	performing	

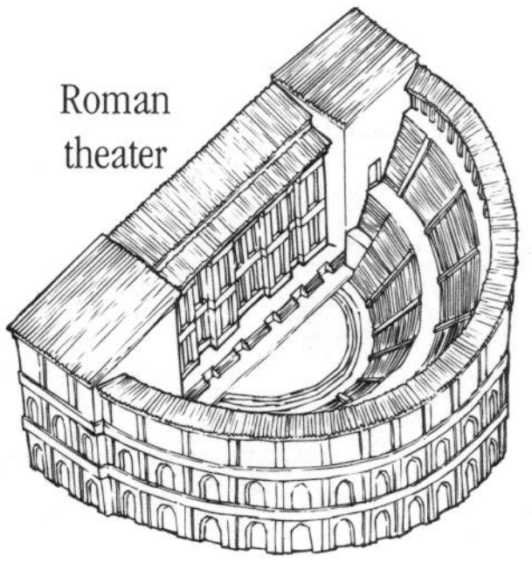

Roman theater

The _____ [1] of theater date back to around 500 B.C., perhaps _____ [2].

The Romans borrowed the idea of actors _____ [3] in theaters from Greece and

the best _____ [4] in Rome were usually Greeks. The first stage shows were

_____ [5] during religious festivals. Actors wore light

_____ [6] which indicated the _____ [7] they

were playing—young children or old _____ [8], gods or goddesses, villains or

_____ [9]. The masks had eye holes and also _____ [10] holes for the actors

to _____ [11] through. Romans from all classes _____ [12] the theater though

actors weren't highly thought of by _____ [13] citizens. Many actors were trained _____ [14] or

freedmen controlled by a manager. The _____ [15] could watch dramas, but _____ [16]

plays with songs and _____ [17] were the most popular. Roman pantomimes had an

_____ [18] dancing and miming a _____ [19] story while others sang or played

_____ [20] like cymbals, pipes, castanets and _____ [21]. Unlike today,

pipes

actors in mimes had _____ [22] roles. Rome's wealthy citizens could

_____ [23] to pay for artistic performances by actors, singers and _____ [24].

horn

They were held at home to _____ [25] families and guests.

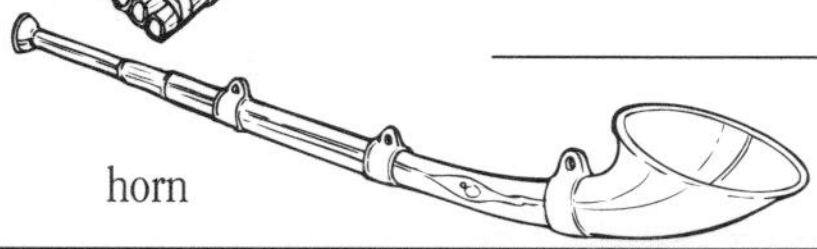

Activity Box

2. Follow the procedure and make your own actor's mask.

   (a) Cut out the shape of your mask in card stock. Make eye/mouth holes.

   (b) Build up your mask with papier-mâché. Make sure cheeks, eyebrows, chin and lips are built up high so they can be seen from a distance.

   (c) If you are going to use a stick to hold your mask (as in the diagram, top right), fix it in place on the back.

   (d) While it is drying out, fix the mask in a curved position so it will fit around your face.

   (e) Paint your mask with vivid colors and when it is dry, give it two coats of varnish.

ROMAN LIFE – ENTERTAINMENT (4)

Children's Games

Children played a variety of games but artwork and mosaics often show them playing with pets, especially dogs and birds.

Apart from in Pompeii and Rome, children's toys have been found in various parts of the Empire and some, like rag dolls, have been well preserved in the dry soils of hot regions like Egypt. Shopkeepers today would not be able to sell some of the toys found in excavations as they were made from lead, a poisonous metal. Small, unearthed models of chariots tell us that Roman children were as interested as their parents in chariot races.

Hoops were made of slender branches that would bend without breaking and had ties to hold their shapes. Other hoops were made of iron or bronze.

Archaeologists have found the ancient remains of see-saws, rocking horses and dolls' houses in excavations in Rome. These toys were usually only provided for children of wealthy families, but it appears that Roman children, rich and poor, played games like hide and seek, blindman's buff and leapfrog, for they are portrayed in Roman art. These games, of course, required no expensive equipment.

Riding a small carriage drawn by a dog, sheep, or goat was a favorite children's pastime. Much smaller versions drawn by model horses, birds, or other wild or domestic animals were popular toys.

Children played checkers or built things with building bricks rather than the wooden or plastic blocks used by children today.

One of the biggest festivals of the year was the Saturnalia in late December, believed to be the origin of our Christmas celebrations. During this time, schools were closed and children were even allowed to play gambling games.

ROMAN LIFE – ENTERTAINMENT (4)

Children's Games

We know about the games Roman children played from murals, relief sculptures and Roman writings. Children flew kites, rolled hoops, spun tops, walked on stilts and played ball games. Handball against a wall was very popular with adults and children. Boys played war games and fought with wooden swords while girls played with dolls made of rags, clay, or wax. Some dolls even had jointed legs and arms. All children played a game similar to marbles where the marbles were made of glass or pottery. Walnuts or pebbles were also used. Knucklebones was popular and played with pieces of pottery or small bones from goats and sheep. Poor children worked long hours but still found time to play games for most could not read or write. The children of wealthy citizens had slaves working for them so they had plenty of time to play or invent games.

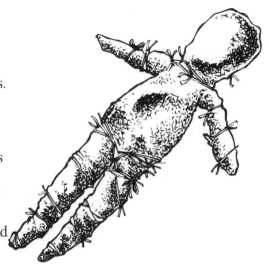

1. Capita and Navia (Heads and tails)

This was played at Saturnalia, a festival around Christmas. Two coins are tossed and the player guesses "two heads," "two tails," or "head and tails." During the Imperial years a coin had the emperor's head on one side and often a ship on the reverse side.

2. Roll the Dice

Two dice are rolled and the player with the higher number has a win.

3. Micatio

One partner puts both hands behind his back. On a signal from his opponent he brings out both hands with one, two, three, four, or five fingers extended on each hand. As one player shows his hands the other player shouts out a number from 2 to 10. The player who correctly guesses the total number of extended fingers has a win.

4. Par Impar ("odd or even")

One child holds stones, coins, or walnuts in a closed hand. The other player has to guess whether the number of objects is odd or even.

5. Tossing game

Throwing nuts into a narrow-necked jar from a set distance.

Activity Box

Set up the 5 games listed above. Nominate each child as a red, white, blue, or green member of a team like the chariot racing teams. Then pair off and play a different partner in each game. To win a match, a player must be the first to reach 10 winning guesses/plays or the player leading after a set time. Record the wins for each color on a class graph to find the winning team.

FARMING

"O tillers of the soil, most happy men!" said the great Roman poet Virgil as he described farmers. But many farm workers were prisoners of war who became slaves working on the country estates of wealthy patrician Roman families. The Punic Wars against the Carthaginians had provided Rome with many slaves, but cultivation of the land by slave workers gradually changed over the years. In time, free men began to produce crops on tenant farms rented from landowners. Female slaves were freed and encouraged to produce large families to provide future farm workers.

As the Romans became undisputed rulers of the Mediterranean region, the opportunity to acquire slaves by waging war against neighboring nations was greatly reduced because of the prevailing peace. As a result, the number of huge farming estates with hundreds of slaves gradually declined.

In the Mediterranean climate regions there were heavy winter rains, so Roman farmers had to ensure their fields were well drained. They dug drainage ditches across their land and filled them with twigs or stones.

The farmers in conquered nations had to grow more crops for they also had to provide food for the Roman troops in their area and sell any surplus food to pay taxes to the emperor. The huge quantities of grain needed for Rome's own population meant a lot had to be imported from various provinces in the Empire, especially Egypt.

Hazel and willow trees were grown to provide slender stems for basketry work and temperate zone trees like beech, oak and elm were used for charcoal burning or timber for construction purposes.

FARMING

In early Roman times, the land was owned by the State and by private owners. The land had been surveyed and divided up into small farms and large estates owned by wealthy landowners. The small farms were worked by the farmer and his sons, for women didn't usually work in the fields.

After the wars against Carthage ended around 200 B.C., Rome regained control of Italy, but many farmers serving in the Roman army had died in battle and their farms had been destroyed. When the State sold the land, only the rich could afford the price and the labor required to repair the damage, so huge farming estates with large villas developed over the years. These estates were worked by slaves and though some estate owners looked after their workers, most slaves worked very long hours in all weather conditions. Some were eventually set free when they were too old to work.

Most Romans made their living through agriculture, and Marcus Cato, a famous soldier-politician, remarked that the most profitable farming was growing vines for wines and olives for olive oil.

Raising sheep and cattle and growing grain were other important farm activities. Sheep were bred mainly for wool and around the Mediterranean, were used to produce milk and cheese.

The farmers irrigated their land and fertilized it with animal manure. They kept cattle, sheep, goats and pigs and noticed that the soil was more fertile where animals grazed on the land. Crops like wheat, barley, beans, turnips and cabbage were rotated, with some fields also left fallow to recover. A wide range of vegetables was grown throughout the Empire, along with fruit like peaches, plums, grapes and cherries and nuts, which included almonds, walnuts, hazelnuts and chestnuts.

Activity Box

1. Who didn't work in the fields on farms?

   _____

2. Which two activities did Cato say gave farmers most profit?

   _____

3. Which animals were used to make milk and cheese?

   _____

4. How did farmers enrich their land?

   _____

5. How would you have treated your slaves had you been a rich landowner?

   _____

   _____

   _____

6. Color in the picture of slave farm workers in the vineyard of a rich man's estate with the villa in the background.

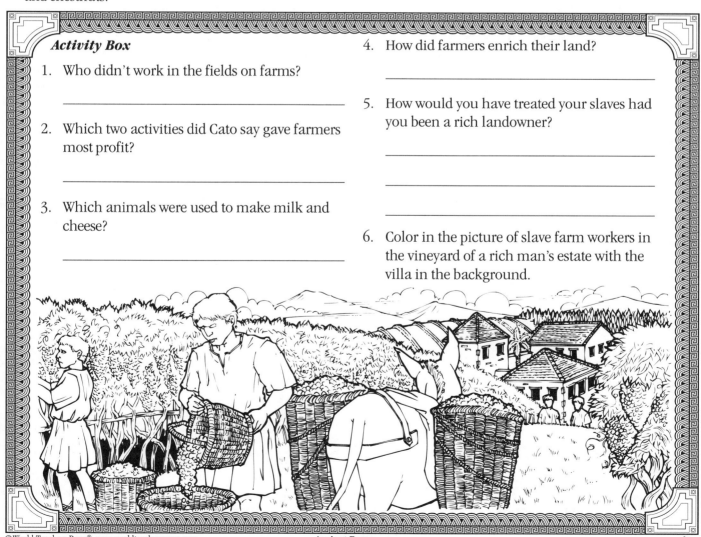

FARMING – TOOLS (1)

There was no rapid development of more sophisticated farming tools during the expansion of the Roman Empire, as there was an abundance of slaves from conquered nations and they carried out all the manual work. Thus, labor-saving devices were not a priority.

The simple plow, which only made a furrow for the seeds, was gradually improved during the years of the Empire, probably by the Romans. The heavier wet soils of northern regions of the Empire meant that a heavy coulter blade was added to break up the soil, which was then turned over by the plowshare behind it. Seeds were then planted by hand from a basket.

The scythe with an iron blade was used for cutting corn. The sickle was also used, but because it had a short handle, using it would have been back-breaking work for farm slaves. The iron prongs in a rake were usually fixed into a strong wood like oak. The turf cutter was used by soldiers constructing defenses around forts in the various regions of the Empire. Tools like these were excavated from the remains of a fort in Scotland. Repairs to tools with iron parts were done by metalworkers who would set up their own furnaces.

A Roman innovation was to combine two tools in one—a pick with a spade.

"Some land, when you have plowed it with oxen and plow, must be plowed again before you plant the seed."

This comment was by Marcus Varrao, a famous first century B.C. Roman writer whose books on farming have survived intact. He referred to a Roman method that involved repeated plowing in a criss-cross pattern to break the ground into fine soil particles. Oxen were the most common draft animals for plows and carts.

Activity Suggestion

The class could be asked to compare (written work/diagrams) examples of modern farm tools/machinery with those used in Roman times.

FARMING – TOOLS (1)

The only machine used in the fields of Roman farms was the plow. All the other tasks on the land were done by hand with tools similar to those used on farms hundreds of years later.

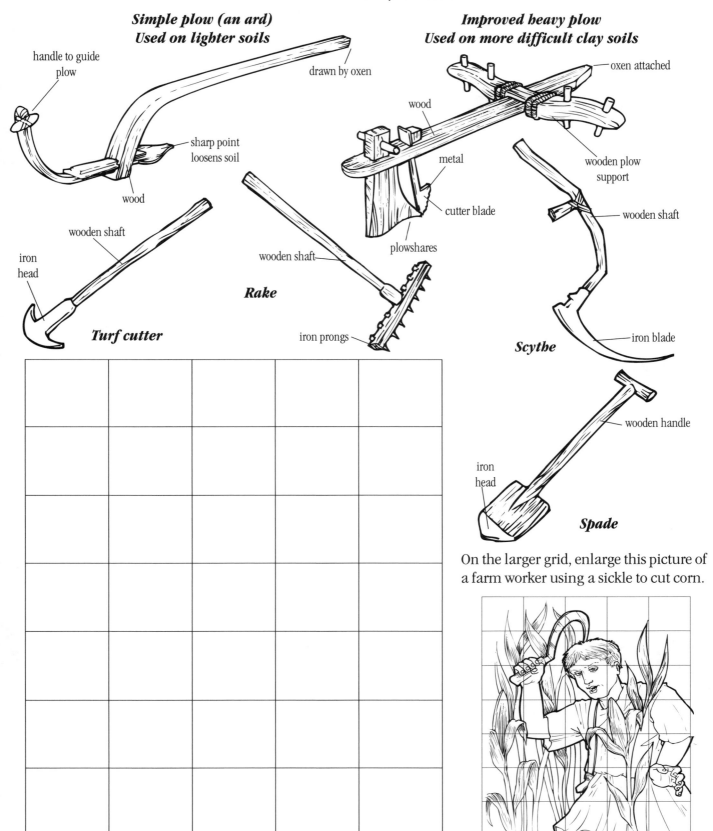

Simple plow (an ard)
Used on lighter soils

handle to guide plow

drawn by oxen

sharp point loosens soil

wood

Improved heavy plow
Used on more difficult clay soils

oxen attached

wood

metal

wooden plow support

cutter blade

plowshares

wooden shaft

wooden shaft

iron head

Turf cutter

wooden shaft

Rake

iron prongs

Scythe

iron blade

wooden handle

iron head

Spade

On the larger grid, enlarge this picture of a farm worker using a sickle to cut corn.

FARMING – TOOLS (2)

See page 68 for Farming – Tools background information and teacher's notes.

Additional Activities

1. Discuss how the use of slaves and the primitive farming tools are linked? Without the use of slaves, would the development of technolgy have been quicker in these times?

   Note: The use of slaves provided a source of labor that did not require payment, which produced a false economy for the farming process.

2. Discuss how the design of basic farming implements such as the spade, rake and turf cutter have not changed. Why is this?

FARMING – TOOLS (2)

Compare the farming tools of Ancient Rome with those used today. Collect pictures or draw examples of the modern comparison.

Simple plow (an ard) ***Used on lighter soils***	
Improved heavy plow ***Used on more difficult*** ***clay soils***	
Turf cutter	
Rake	
Scythe	
Spade	

TRADE

The Romans advanced their road-building skills by improving the methods employed by the Etruscans and the Greeks. They built roads which were generally straight, with good foundations and hard-wearing surfaces. The roads had tunnels, embankments and bridges and the Romans cleared bushes and trees alongside roads in the conquered provinces to prevent surprise attacks on their soldiers.

Roads which have been excavated show no standard design. The foundations were similar but surfaces varied, with gravel, pebbles, or cut stone slabs being used. The roads had a slight curve (camber) to assist drainage. The road widths varied from around one meter to nine meters, depending on their importance.

Merchant ships had sails because oars would need too many crew members for rowing. Unlike the oared warships, merchant vessels had to be towed out of a harbor in order to catch the wind. They were navigated by the stars at night and used landmarks and the direction of the wind by day.

Pirates often pillaged merchant ships but their main profits came from slave-trading. For this reason wealthy Romans may have discouraged action against pirates as they needed the slaves. Threats against the Roman trade in imported grain eventually led to Pompey's action.

The Emperor Augustus levied taxes on imports with exemptions on animals, soldiers' equipment and property of the emperor. Taxes were collected at town gates, important road junctions, bridges and ports. A tax would normally be about 2.5%, but could be as high as 25%.

Spices like coriander, nutmeg, ginger and pepper were important as they disguised the flavor of food that wasn't fresh. When Alaric the Visigoth laid siege to Rome he asked for 3,000 pounds of pepper as part of his demands.

Roman coins were consistent in weight and quality despite the fact they were coined under different rulers whose heads were stamped on one side. In time, the Romans did not favor the continual provision of coins to the Far East, for they recycled the gold and silver in them, so export restrictions were introduced. Eventually, Indian traders lost confidence because of the reduced supply and began to barter with quality goods like gems and linen for Roman ceramics and wine.

TRADE

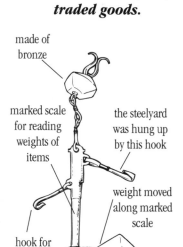

For many years during the "Pax Romana" (the Roman peace), the Empire all around the Mediterranean Sea was a huge region of peace and stability, so trade between countries flourished. The vast Roman road systems, which eventually covered around 90,000 km, were built to move their soldiers quickly from place to place but they were also a huge benefit to growing trade for they enabled carts drawn by oxen and horses to travel easily between towns.

Roman ships traveled the world and Ostia, the port of Rome, unloaded grain from Egypt, silk from China, perfumes and cotton along with spices like pepper from India, wines from Spain, precious stones from around the Mediterranean and ivory, gold and wild beasts from North Africa for the amphitheaters. Roman ports like Ostia had stone lighthouses to guide the ships. The guiding light at night came from fires in braziers inside the building while mirrors to reflect the sun's rays were used during the day.

Trading ships sailed the seas mainly in summer to avoid winter storms, but had to contend with pirates. Roman warships protected the main shipping routes until Pompey, a military leader, cleared the Mediterranean of pirates around 67 B.C.

Merchant ship

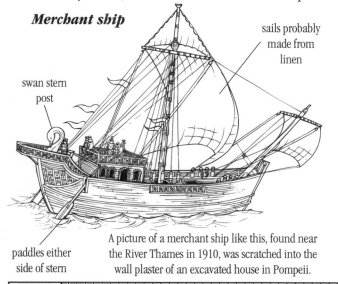

sails probably made from linen

swan stern post

paddles either side of stern

A picture of a merchant ship like this, found near the River Thames in 1910, was scratched into the wall plaster of an excavated house in Pompeii.

Merchant ships didn't have compasses so they usually hugged the coast. Some were lost in storms and shipwrecks have been found with 10,000 amphorae containing oil or wine.

The spread of trade during the peace helped to carry clothing fashions, building methods, new ideas and Christianity from its origins in the Middle East. Most people used goods produced in their local area but wealthy Roman citizens wanted exotic luxury goods from distant lands with cultures different from their own. Alexandria in Egypt was the main port through which goods from the Far East passed and the merchants there were mainly Greek. The Romans paid for the goods they bought with gold or silver coins which have been unearthed in places as far away as East Africa, Britain and Vietnam.

Activity Box

1. Why did trading ships sail mainly in summer? _____

2. How do we know trading ships visited Britain? _____

3. What problem on the trade routes was solved by Pompey? _____

4. What was used to guide ships during the day? _____

5. Why did merchant ships keep close to the coast? _____

6. Why do you think there were many peaceful years in the Empire around the Mediterranean?

   _____

7. On a separate sheet of paper, draw some goods imported by Roman merchant ships.

ROMAN TECHNOLOGY – AQUEDUCTS

The Romans began to build aqueducts around 312 B.C. in order to carry water to Rome, but the ancient Assyrians had constructed an aqueduct about 400 years before that date to provide water for the city of Ninevah. Ten main aqueducts carried a continuous flow of water to Rome. One of them, the Aqua Claudia, carried spring water from the Appenine mountains and its ruins can still be seen today. Most of the Aqua Claudia was underground so the water could not be accidentally contaminated or deliberately fouled by Rome's dissatisfied poorer citizens. The underground channels were normally only half filled with water so there was room to remove the deposits of calcium carbonate which narrowed the channels and restricted the water flow.

The Pont du Gard Aqueduct in Southern France ran for about 50 km and supplied water to the city of Nimes. It was built by Marcus Agrippa, an engineer and soldier, and stood 48 meters above a valley. Another aqueduct rises above Segovia in Spain, but the most impressive in Roman times was one which carried water across mountains and desert to the city of Carthage in North Africa. Its length was over 200 km and many sections still stand today.

Roman plumbing used many lead pipes and tanks and even then a brilliant engineer called Marcus Vitruvius was sounding a warning about the danger to health of lead in water. The common alternative was ceramic pipes built in sections and then linked together. The joints were sealed with a mixture of quicklime and oil.

In 1850, Paris engineers were still using aspects of a water supply system worked out by Frontinus, a Roman aqueduct designer.

Activity Suggestion

A model could be made to show that though aqueducts took years to build, the concept was quite a simple one.

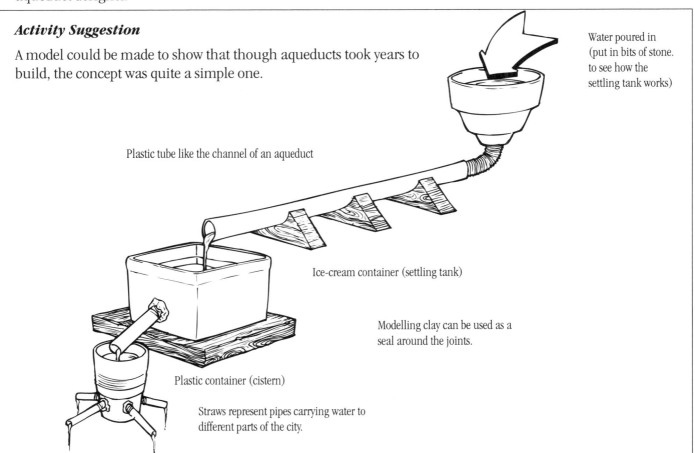

Water poured in (put in bits of stone. to see how the settling tank works)

Plastic tube like the channel of an aqueduct

Ice-cream container (settling tank)

Modelling clay can be used as a seal around the joints.

Plastic container (cistern)

Straws represent pipes carrying water to different parts of the city.

ROMAN TECHNOLOGY – AQUEDUCTS

This Roman aqueduct still stands in France and took years to build. It is raised up high on an arched bridge and the blocks of stone fit so tightly no mortar was used to hold them together. Some blocks weigh over 5 tons and were raised into position by cranes powered by slaves on treadmills.

Supplies of water are needed by any community. Villages and small towns can obtain water from wells, springs and streams. As Roman cities developed in a region where drought was often a problem, more sophisticated ways of supplying water were needed. The Romans believed that polluted water harmed the health of their citizens so they developed a system which used aqueducts and sewers to keep the people healthy.

Aqueducts could be built at ground level as channels cut through rock or below the ground using pipes. Pipes were difficult to clean and probably more expensive than aqueduct bridges with simple channels if ongoing maintenance was taken into account. Wherever possible, Roman engineers used gravity to carry water from a source to a city. Such aqueducts were built up high on huge arches of brick and stone and sloped down from the water source. The slope had to be very gradual if the source was some distance from the community. In Rome, they carried millions of liters of water daily into the public baths, fountains and homes of the wealthy citizens. Householders had to pay for the water supplied with payments based on the diameter of the pipe delivering the water. Water from the aqueduct first flowed into settling tanks where sand and other sediment settled to the bottom.

There were excellent sewerage systems in Rome, some still in use today. Large stone tunnels would flush waste products into the River Tiber, using flowing water brought in along aqueducts.

Activity Box

Answers to the questions are found above.

1. What are settling tanks for?

   _____

2. Why were aqueducts often built at a high point?

   _____

3. How were rich citizens charged for water?

   _____

   _____

4. The Romans used aqueducts to clean out waste products in …

   _____.

5. Name the original water sources mentioned.

   _____

6. Water was important to Rome for the region often suffered from …

   _____.

7. Where would Rome's sewage end up?

   _____

8. What were the important curved structures in the aqueduct?

   _____

9. What did the Romans believe harmed their health?

   _____

10. Which part of the aqueduct system would have been difficult to maintain?

   _____

ROMAN TECHNOLOGY

Coffer Dam

These were built in the northern regions of the Empire where rivers did not dry up. In hot regions, bridge piers could be built on dry riverbeds in summer. The piers were well-spaced so the water didn't rush through narrow gaps and erode them. Some piers were roughly triangular in shape with the apex facing upstream so water would flow around them easily.

Concrete walls

Using a reddish volcanic earth called pozzolana, which was mixed with limestone and water, the Romans could make a strong cement. This was then mixed with sand and crushed stones to make concrete. In Emperor Hadrian's reign, some walls were made of concrete mixed with travertine, a local stone quarried near Rome. After the great fire in Rome during Emperor Nero's reign, it was found that brick-faced concrete was more fire-resistant and this discovery led to more brickyards being built.

The kiln

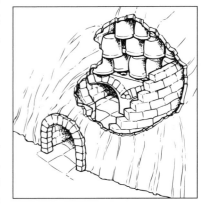

Clay was used to make bricks, tiles, pipes and other kiln-fired objects like figurines, lamps and candlesticks. Pottery was made by hand or on a potter's wheel and dried before firing. An updraft kiln had a hole in the roof where sometimes layers of turf closed in the domed roof. More sophisticated kilns were used for "terra sigillata" (clay decorated with figures). Amphorae for holding wine or oil were often made leakproof by coating the inside with a distilled resin made from pine trees. Before firing, many bricks or tiles were stamped with the name of the army unit that made them. Large amounts of limestone and chalk were burned in kilns to provide lime for making mortar.

The arch

The arch was conceived by the Egyptians and Greeks. When the keystone was dropped into place it locked the arch together and the downward pressure was spread around the arch and onto the two supporting piers. The wooden semicircular frame had to be strong enough to support the arch until the mortar set. The Romans employed the arch concept to construct vaulted roofs and domes.

Suggested Activity

The Romans pressed clay into molds. Students could press small pieces of clay into a shallow dish, making sure the pieces overlap and an even thickness is maintained so they won't crack when fired. After pressing, the top can be evened off by cutting the surplus away with fishing line. Allow to dry out for a few days and the clay will shrink and should come out easily.

ROMAN TECHNOLOGY

The Romans were responsible for very few important inventions but have often improved on the technology of other nations for they were fine engineers. They did not develop many labor-saving ideas because they had a plentiful supply of slave and animal power.

Activity Box

Use the given words to fill in the gaps in the notes.

(a)   **circles   dug   water   enclosure   support   beds   clay   pumped**

The Romans could build piers to _____[1] bridge

arches in the _____[2] of rivers. An

_____[3] was made with two concentric

_____[4] of wooden piles.

Then _____[5] was used between the piles and

the _____[6] in the middle was

_____[7] or bailed out. The soft river

bed was _____[8] out and the concrete pier built.

A Coffer Dam

1. Logs driven into river bed
2. Wickerwork to hold in the clay
3. Clay filled gap

4. Middle section filled with concrete after water pumped out of center
5. The concrete then forms the base for an arch of a bridge.

(b)   **faced   sand   hardened   Romans   bricks   Timber   support   mixture**

Concrete is a _____[1] of cement, water,

stones and _____[2] first used by the

_____[3] in 200 B.C.

_____[4] was used to

_____[5] the wall until the concrete

_____[6]. The concrete core was then

_____[7] with stones or

_____[8] after it had set.

Concrete shoveled in

Roman Wall

Stones or bricks

Scaffolding for workers and to support wall as concrete sets

Roman Arch

wooden support frame

(c)   **frame   invent   stones   side   top   strong   keystone   wedges**

The Romans didn't _____[1] the arch but they realized how

_____[2] it was. Large _____[3] shaped like

_____[4] were built up on either _____[5]

around a wooden _____[6] until the final _____[7]

was locked into place at the _____[8] of the arch.

ROMAN WOMEN

Young women had no say in selecting a husband. A girl was often married by the age of 13 or 14 and her parents gave a dowry of money and goods to her future husband. If she became a widow, she regained control of her dowry. Dowries were an expected custom but not legal requirements.

The position of women in society did improve after Augustus became the first Roman emperor in 27 B.C. and some educated women became teachers and doctors. During the Imperial Age, the time of the emperors, women could own land, run businesses, free slaves and make wills. These were privileges they didn't have in early Rome.

Wealthy women used ivory combs but the poor used combs made of wood or bone, mainly to remove hair lice. The teeth in combs like those made from bone were cut with a very fine saw.

Olive oil was used in the preparation of soap, skin oils and perfumes. Perfume jars were ceramic, carved from marble or made from blown glass. Some glass cosmetic jars had gold bands running through the lids, probably floated in when the glass was in liquid form.

In the first and second centuries A.D., elaborate female hairstyles were very popular, with curls or braids piled up high on a wire framework. Wigs were sometimes made from the blond hair of northern European men captured in battles with Roman legions.

Clothing for men and women did not change a lot over the centuries. Women in early Rome wore togas like men, but in later times wore tunics and robes, as togas became associated with women of ill-repute. Children usually wore small versions of adult clothing.

Mirrors were often made of polished metals like bronze or silver, as the use of reflective glass in mirrors had not been invented.

ROMAN WOMEN

Items used by Roman women.

Bronze mirror

Ivory comb found in a grave

Perfume jar

Bone needle and thimble

Tweezers

Though women had few career opportunities and usually looked after and organized their household, wives of men in important positions, like senators, often had a lot of influence in private. In the early Republic, apart from working in the home or shop, rich women could become priestesses or run their own businesses, but it was usually only the men who could work in the professions. Women could not become magistrates or vote in elections and had no legal rights over children.

Though rich women had money to spend on expensive lotions to hide the aging process, their life expectancy was only about 30 years, compared with around 80 years today. Many Roman women died in childbirth but some did survive to old age. Poor women, like thousands of female slaves, had little time or money to spend on their appearance, but wealthy women were very particular about theirs. Cosmetics were made from a variety of natural products. To soften the skin, a cream made from wheat flour and milk from a donkey was used. White skin was popular and was whitened with a paste of white lead or powdered chalk.

Wigs were worn and slaves would help to curl their mistress's hair with heated tongs. Like men, women dyed their hair blonde or a variety of colors and then scented it with perfumed oil. Common jewelry items were made of bronze or glass but many necklaces, robe clasps, bracelets and earrings worn by rich women were made from gold or precious stones. Men and women wore similar clothes. Women wore tunics with long robes over them and the clothes were made of wool or linen, silk if they were rich. They sometimes wore underclothes of soft leather and brightly colored sandals made of tougher leather.

Activity Box

1. How did clothes worn by rich women differ from those worn by poor women?

   _____

2. Name two rights a woman didn't have.

   _____

   _____

3. What do you think of the life of women in early Rome?

   _____

   _____

   _____

4. Solve the puzzle using words from the notes.

Across

2. Not many
5. Frequently
6. Olive product
7. Brooches
10. Wealthy
12. Liquid preparations
13. Smooth cloth
14. Lowly workers

Down

1. Wheat product
3. Animal hair
4. Assist
7. Type of limestone
8. Alike
9. Perfumed
11. Hairpieces

ROMAN LIFE – LANGUAGE

There was no coercion to make the people of conquered nations speak Latin, but the wealthy citizens of those provinces were encouraged to speak the language as part of the Romanization process adopted in conquered countries. Native languages such as Celtic ("Keltik") and Punic were still spoken and Latin had little influence in regions of the Eastern Empire where Greek was the main language.

In a time before printing machines were invented, the written language was not familiar to ordinary citizens, apart from inscriptions on public monuments, temples and graves. Books were written by hand and, as they often took many months to complete, they were very expensive and out of the reach of poor families.

Thousands of Latin inscriptions have been unearthed over the years and a pile of letters preserved in a Scottish well shows that some ordinary Roman soldiers could read and write.

After the end of the Empire, Latin continued to be used in churches and is still part of religious ceremonies today, especially Roman Catholic services. Even after the barbarian invasions of the fifth century A.D. which destroyed the Western Empire, Latin continued to be the main language of communication in the western regions of the Empire.

ROMAN LIFE – LANGUAGE

MOBELLIO·MI·FIRMO·AED·ILL
II·VIR·ID·H·VIC·DECVRIONES·LOC·
SEPVLIVR·ALFTINIVNLR·HSI·CENSVER·PAGAN
THVF·ISFXXX·FFCIVPEVM·MINN·REORINODORIFIF·CO·ETCFVPEVM

Inscription from Pompeii showing the
differentia and accents marking long vowels.

As the Empire spread throughout the known world, different languages were spoken within its borders. However, the official language was Latin, which helped to unite the various regions. Wealthy Romans also learned Greek at school or from tutors. A reasonable number of ordinary citizens, especially those in cities, could read and write Latin, as revealed in workmen's accounts, simple letters and even graffiti on walls. In fact, over 3,500 examples of graffiti have been found on the walls of Pompeii.

The Romans introduced writing to northern Europe and most modern European languages are based on the Latin alphabet.

The alphabet had only 22 letters; there was no "W" or "Y" and both "I" and "J" were written as "I," and "V" and "U" written as "V." Punctuation and spacing between words were rarely used and there were no initial capital letters in sentences. Differentia (stops) usually divided words on inscriptions but were often put in the wrong place. These stops could be decorative, in the shape of ivy leaves, for example.

Activity Box

Many of our words are derived from Latin, a language still taught in some educational institutions. Use your dictionary to find the English derivations from the Roman words.

Roman Word (Latin)	Meaning of Latin Word	Meaning of English word	English Word
1. Bestiarius	animal fighter	an animal	
2. Decem	ten	tenth month on Roman calendar	
3. Mars	God of war	related to war or soldiers	
4. Vigila	wake up!	alert, prepared	
5. Pedes	feet	a foot lever	
6. Gladius	sword	plant with swordlike leaves	
7. Navis	a ship	a fleet of ships	
8. Domus	a house	relating to a home	
9. Tepidarium	warm room in a public baths	lukewarm	
10. Volumen	papyrus sheets glued together	a book	
11. Vale	goodbye	a farewell speech	
12. Salarium	money paid to Roman soldiers to buy salt	wages	
13. Praefectus	Roman official	someone with authority	
14. Aquila	the eagle on a Roman standard	like an eagle	
15. Princeps	a chief	the head of an institution	
16. Maritus	husband	relating to marriage	

ROMAN LIFE – NUMBERS

The early Roman number system of around 500 B.C. was different in some respects from the system we use in schools today. At that time, a Roman wrote 4 as IIII (not IV) and 9 as VIIII (not IX).

The older Roman numeral for 100 was ⊖ with ⊕ and ⊗ also being used. 1,000 was written as ⏀ or ⏀ or ◁|▷. M as the symbol for 1,000 was rarely used until it became more common hundreds of years later.

The Romans were not particularly interested in mathematics. They had little use for large numbers and avoided the use of fractions.

There are several theories regarding the shape of the numerals. The 1 is believed to represent a finger, the V possibly the shape between the forefinger and thumb or the rough shape of the five fingers. The X is thought to be the two hands joined and the C is probably an abbreviation for "centum" which is Latin for one hundred. The numeral L was written ⌄ or ⊥ during the years of the Republic and the D usually had a middle bar (Đ). The Roman numeral for 500 (D) is believed to be derived from the bisection of the old symbol for 1,000 (⏀).

The problems using the additive and subtractive principles may need some chalkboard practice first.

Ancient Rome

ROMAN LIFE – NUMBERS

Roman numerals (symbols representing numbers) are better known today than the numerals of any other ancient number systems, such as the Greek or Egyptian. The Roman system was based on seven numerals, which were I, V, X, L, C, D and M. Like our numbers they were written from left to right, but there was no place value as we have in our system. We have the commonly used values, thousands, hundreds, tens and units, so two thousand,

three hundred and sixty-eight can be shown as 2 3 6 8. The same number using Roman numerals would be MMCCCLXVIII! Large numbers were clumsy and complicated, and though additions and subtractions were easy to do, other calculations were difficult. As you can see, some numerals can be repeated in a number but "V" and "L" are never repeated.

Towards the end of the Republic in the first century B.C., a bar over a number multiplied it by a thousand, so $\overline{V}$ was 5,000 and $\overline{D}$, 500,000. There was no numeral for zero and centuries later, during the middle ages, Europeans replaced the Roman system with the Hindu-Arabic system which used the symbols 0—9. This made calculations much simpler.

Activity Box

Roman numerals use the additive and subtractive principles. e.g., VII=5+1+1=7 (A), IV = take 1 from 5 = 4(S), XXIV = 10+10+(5-1)=24 (A and S)

1. Complete the examples as shown above. e.g., XXI = 10 + 10 + 1 = 21 (A)

    (a) XI   = _____ = _____ (_____)

    (b) LX   = _____ = _____ (_____)

    (c) XXXIX   = _____ = _____ (_____)

    (d) MCC   = _____ = _____ (_____)

    (e) XC   = _____ = _____ (_____)

    (f) XL   = _____ = _____ (_____)

    (g) CLX   = _____ = _____ (_____)

    (h) DCC   = _____ = _____ (_____)

    (i) MCLIV   = _____ = _____ (_____)

    (j) MDCCC   = _____ = _____ (_____)

2. Now write these Roman numerals from the first century B.C. in our Hindu-Arabic numerals.

    (a) $\overline{L}$ = _____   (g) $\overline{LX}$ = _____

    (b) $\overline{C}$ = _____   (h) $\overline{XC}$ = _____

    (c) $\overline{VI}$ = _____   (i) $\overline{LXX}$ = _____

    (d) $\overline{XVI}$ = _____   (j) $\overline{LV}$ = _____

    (e) $\overline{DC}$ = _____   (k) $\overline{X}$ = _____

    (f) $\overline{M}$ = _____   (l) $\overline{XX}$ = _____

ROMAN NUMBERS GAME

Activity Suggestion

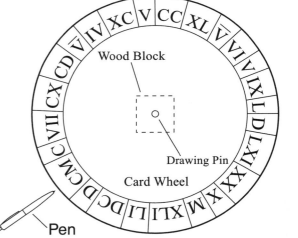

1. Both players estimate their likely score for 10 spins.

2. A ballpoint pen is placed in position.

3. Player "A" spins the wheel and scores the number opposite the pen if the number is read correctly.

4. Player "B" spins the wheel.

5. Players add up their scores and the difference between a player's estimate and actual score is recorded on a class block graph.

Discuss the results.

The "Spin the Roman Wheel" results on the class graph could be discussed with the following questions:

1. Are there any small differences showing good estimates?

2. Did anyone estimate their actual score?

3. Could students be 100% sure their estimates would be correct? Why?

ROMAN NUMBERS GAME

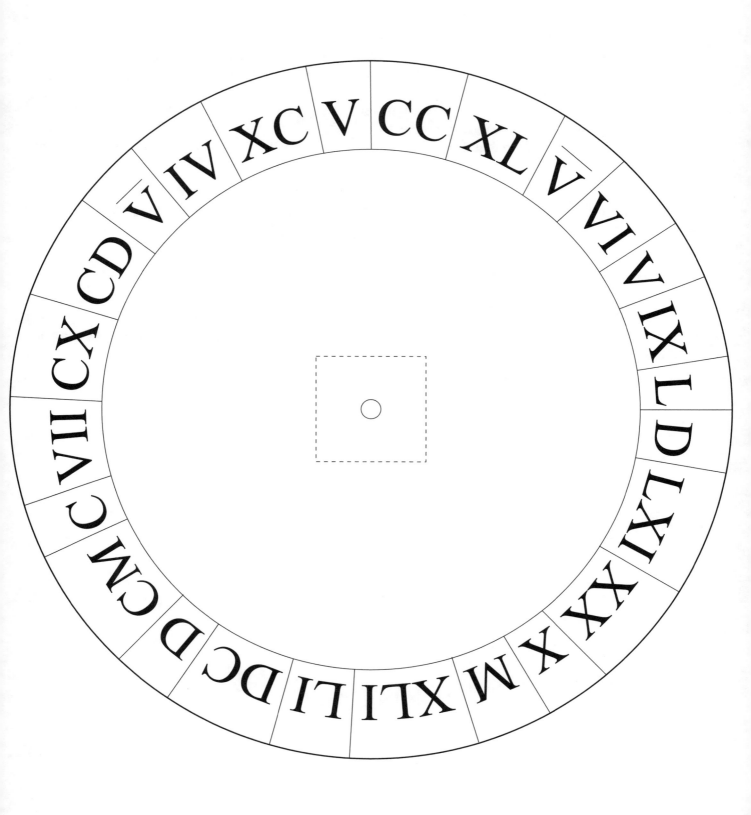

ROMANS IN BRITAIN

Julius Caesar was a great Roman general who served the normal year in office as a consul in 59 B.C. before fighting and defeating the tribes in Gaul. In 55 B.C., his army landed in Kent and advanced inland. He captured hostages but soon sailed back to Gaul after repairing ships damaged in a storm. In 54 B.C., his army advanced over 150 km inland. He vanquished Cassivellaunus, the most important tribal leader, but after taking prisoners and money he returned to Gaul. Some historians believe that Caesar invaded Britain because it was supposed to be rich in minerals and pearls, which may account for his quick departure.

Claudius's army was led by Aulus Plautius, one of his best generals. Plautius captured Colchester, the stronghold of the leading British tribe, but the tribal leader, Caractacus, fled to Wales. He was captured later and taken to Rome to be executed, but Claudius was so impressed by a speech Caractacus made, he was pardoned. Plautius became the first governor of Roman Britain.

Claudius needed the victory in Britain to establish himself as a worthy emperor after the murder of the Emperor Caligula.

In a struggle for power with other generals, Caesar was victorious in the civil wars which followed. He then began to act as the dictator of Rome and made enemies in the Senate, the council that legally ruled Rome. Because some leading Romans wanted Rome to stay a republic with power shared by more than one person, Caesar was murdered in 44 B.C. by a group of powerful men led by Cassius and Brutus, who were supposed to be friends of the great Roman general.

Our month of July is named after him, and during his years in power he improved communications throughout the Empire by building bridges and roads. He also allowed many prisoners of war to become Roman citizens, which gave them their freedom and legal rights.

ROMANS IN BRITAIN

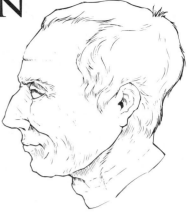

For nearly 400 years, Britain enjoyed the benefits and suffered the cruelties of Roman occupation, until the legions were withdrawn to defend Rome against the Goths.

The first invasion of Britain in 55 B.C. was by Julius Caesar, a military leader of the Roman occupation army in Gaul (France). Caesar believed his enemies in Gaul were aided by Britain so he decided to teach the Britons a lesson. He also wanted further success to gain support against other Roman generals who were his enemies. Caesar invaded again in 54 B.C., but Britain did not become a province until it was invaded and conquered by the emperor Claudius, who sent an army of about 40,000 men in 43 A.D.

Julius Caesar

At this time, Britain was divided into tribal chiefdoms, mainly Celts, who fought each other. Some southern tribes joined together to fight the Romans but were no match for the well-organized army. Several tribes lived in hill forts and an excavation at one fort, Maidstone Castle in Dorset, unearthed a skeleton with a bolt from a Roman ballista lodged in its spine.

A huge fleet of ships was needed to invade Britain and from the time of Claudius there was a Roman fleet in Britain with the main naval bases at Dover and Boulogne in Gaul. There was also a base at Richborough where the Roman invasion force first landed.

Though the Romans captured most of England and Wales and small areas of Scotland, many tribes continued to rebel against them during the years of occupation.

Invasion of Britain in 43 A.D.

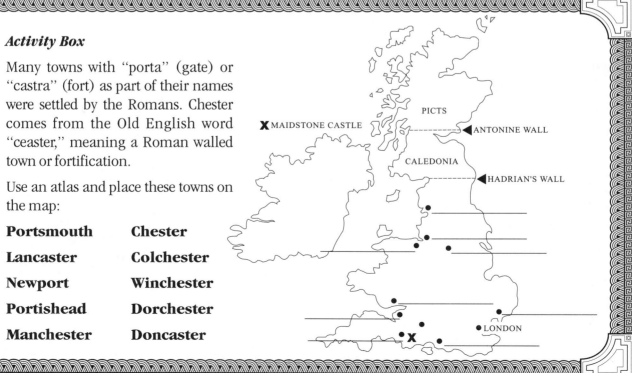

Activity Box

Many towns with "porta" (gate) or "castra" (fort) as part of their names were settled by the Romans. Chester comes from the Old English word "ceaster," meaning a Roman walled town or fortification.

Use an atlas and place these towns on the map:

Portsmouth	**Chester**
Lancaster	**Colchester**
Newport	**Winchester**
Portishead	**Dorchester**
Manchester	**Doncaster**

ROMANS IN BRITAIN – HADRIAN

Trajan, the emperor before Hadrian, expanded the Roman Empire to its greatest size, but Hadrian abandoned Assyria and other conquests in the Eastern Empire except for Arabia, which was then a peaceful province under Roman rule.

Hadrian's Wall was built from Bowness to Newcastle and later extended to Wallsend near the east coast. It was built in front of an older line of forts now known as the Stanegate. The original plan was to house the troops in the Stanegate forts but it was decided to move them into milecastles and larger forts on the wall itself. Eighty milecastles, each holding about 100 soldiers, were built every Roman mile (about 1,480 meters) and between them were watchtowers. (A Roman mile was a thousand paces—the Latin for 1,000 was "mille," the origin of our word "mile.") The new camps encouraged more Britons to join the Roman army and by the end of Hadrian's reign most legionaries were born outside Italy.

Hadrian's Wall varied in height from about 4.5 meters to 6.5 meters. Over a million cubic meters of stone were quarried and carried to the site. Western sections of the wall, west of the Irthing river, were made of turf as limestone for mortar was difficult to obtain. The turf was replaced by stone around 180 A.D. Each legion built a section of about 8 km and when the section was completed an inscribed stone telling who the builders were was built into the wall. The vallum, historians believe, was a military boundary line which civilians could not cross without permission.

In 138 A.D., the emperor Antoninus Pius succeeded Hadrian and he extended the Roman frontier in Britain by building the Antonine wall further north in Scotland.

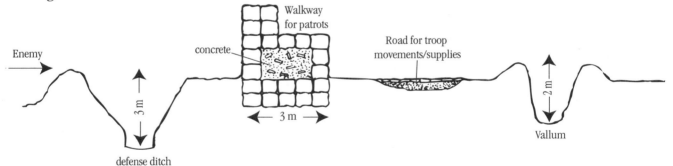

Additional Activity

Read and discuss the poem "The Roman Centurion's Song" by Rudyard Kipling. It tells the story of a Roman soldier who served in Britain for 40 years.

Terms used in Kipling's poem.

Legate — Governor of a Roman province

Portus Itius — Boulogne harbor

Vectis — Isle of Wight

The Wall — Hadrian's Wall

Rhodanus — River Rhone

Nemausus — Roman fortress (Nîmes)

Arelate — Roman town (Arles)

Euroclydon — Stormy wind

Via Aurelia — Road from Rome to Gaul (France)

Tyrrhene Ocean — Part of Mediterranean Sea west of Italy

ROMANS IN BRITAIN – HADRIAN

Hadrian on a denarius (Roman coin). The first emperor to wear a beard.

Hadrian reigned as emperor from 117–138 A.D. Early in his reign he traveled to all parts of the Roman Empire, for he was concerned about security on its borders. Trajan, the great soldier-emperor before him, had wasted men and money on extending the Empire's frontiers. Though an experienced soldier himself, Hadrian believed in a smaller Empire with better defenses against attacks by barbarian tribes. Secure borders enabled the provinces to flourish and provide taxes and tribute (metals, wine, grain) to Rome. Though the two European rivers, the Rhine and Danube, provided natural barriers against the Goths, he built forts between them to keep out the Germanic tribes, but his most famous work was the building of a wall from sea to sea in northern England.

Around 117 A.D., warlike tribes from Caledonia (Scotland) and northern Britannia (Britain) attacked the Romans and caused widespread destruction. After Hadrian's visit to Britain, he thought a huge army was needed to conquer Caledonia and then defend it. In 122 A.D., he ordered a wall to be built to "separate the Romans and the barbarians."

Hadrian's Wall

The wall, partly turf and partly stone, was about 120 km long and took Roman soldiers over five years to build, for the legions had engineers and craftsmen skilled in building fortifications.

Auxiliaries, conquered people who had joined the Roman army, usually manned the wall for the next 250 years. Much of Hadrian's Wall remains today in spite of stones being taken to build local churches, roads and even private homes.

The famous general, Agricola, had defeated the Scottish tribes, but over 100 years later they were still troublesome. The emperor Caracalla later concluded a peace treaty with the Scots and withdrew his armies to Hadrian's Wall, which became Britain's northern border in the third century A.D.

Activity Box

1. Which emperor increased the size of the Roman Empire? _____

2. The Goths were the _____ tribes.

3. Why are there gaps in Hadrian's Wall today? _____

4. Hadrian's Wall was built of stones and _____.

5. What is "tribute"? _____

6. Which seas are at the ends of the Wall? (Atlas needed) _____

7. Who provided services to the Roman troops? _____

8. Why did Caracalla move his army back to Hadrian's Wall? _____

_____

ROMANS IN BRITAIN – BOUDICA

The Roman historian Tacitus (circa 55 A.D. — 120 A.D.) first wrote about the defiant British queen and called her Boudicca.

When his original manuscripts were copied, her name was written wrongly and became Boadicea. This name was accepted for hundreds of years until 20th century scholars discovered the error. Philologists, experts in the authenticity of language in ancient texts, believe that Tacitus was wrong, too, and, the name should only have one "c." Some references still use Boudicca or even Boadicea.

When the King of the Iceni died in about 60 A.D., he left a widow and two daughters. He granted part of his land to the emperor Nero, but a devious Roman official, a procurator responsible for the administration of a Roman province, tried to get extra protection money from the tribe and even stole some of their land. Boudica refused to pay money or allow her land to be confiscated. She was flogged and her daughters reputedly assaulted by Roman soldiers. Boudica then spent her life seeking revenge. When she attacked Roman towns—now Colchester, St. Albans and London—around 70,000 lives were lost. Paullinus (also Paulinus) suggested harsh reprisals against the Iceni after he had defeated Boudica, but Nero recalled him to Rome and appointed more understanding officials.

The savage Iceni tribe once painted themselves with woad, a blue dye made from the flowers and leaves of plants. Though Roman occupation enriched their lives in many ways, Roman greed and brutality led them to rebellion.

ROMANS IN BRITAIN – BOUDICA

"In stature she was very tall, in appearance most terrifying, in the glance of her eye most fierce, and her voice was harsh." – Cassius Dio, ancient Roman historian.

1. Use these words to complete the passage about Boudica.

slew	shields	troops	eastern	swords	invaders	cooperated	drew	tribe
spare	javelins	liberate	governor	Roman	organized	equipped	army	rout
fled	experienced							

Boudica was the warrior-queen of the Iceni, a Celtic _____[1] which first

rebelled against the Romans in 47 A.D. in the _____[2] part of Britain.

She led a huge _____[3] of thousands of supporters against the

_____[4] oppressors in 60 A.D. Boudica attacked Londinium

(London) and did not _____[5] those Britons who had

_____[6] with the Romans. Believing she could

_____[7] her people from the _____[8], she

fought a fierce battle with the disciplined _____[9] of

the Roman military _____[10], Suetonius Paullinus in 61 A.D.

Her army was badly _____[11] and no match for the well

_____[12] Roman legionaries under their _____[13]

general. After flinging their _____[14] the Roman forces _____[15] their short stabbing

_____[16] and, protected by their long _____[17], charged the Britons. The battle now became

a _____[18] as the frightened rebels _____[19] in terror and the pursuing Romans

_____[20] men, women and children.

Note: Rather than being captured by the Romans, Boudica died after taking poison.

Bronze statue of Boudica near the Houses of Parliament, London.

2. List the four adjectives Cassius Dio used to describe Boudica.

   (a) _____

   (b) _____

   (c) _____

   (d) _____

3. How many years was it from the first revolt of the Iceni to their defeat in 61 A.D?

   _____

4. Which word means "an overwhelming defeat"?

   _____

5. How can we tell the Romans were merciless fighters?

   _____

6. Which word in the passage means "to set free"?

   _____

7. Which word tells us Paullinus was a soldier?

   _____

8. What was the name of Boudica's tribe?

   _____

9. Boudica's followers were well armed. True or false?

   _____

ROMANS IN BRITAIN – SOME IMPORTANT SITES

Vindolanda

The first fort on this site was built in 85 A.D. on the Stanegate frontier. The wooden writing tablets were badly decayed but a great deal of the written information has been preserved. The tablets list foods such as garlic, radishes and beans and contain many letters, one of which says "I implore your majesty not to allow me, an innocent man, to be beaten with rods."

Wroxeter

The tombstone inscription tells us it was Marcus Petronius, a 38-year-old soldier of the 14th legion.

Thetford

The quality of the workmanship on the artifacts suggests that they were made in the fourth century A.D.

Corbridge

In the damp British climate, the Romans dried grain in a granary. The grain was strewn on wooden floors laid on top of stone pillars. Air circulating underneath dried the grain.

Bath

People came to swim in the medicinal waters and pray to Sulis, a Celtic goddess the Romans associated with their goddess, Minerva. The baths are still used, but the health-giving waters have recently been contaminated with bacteria.

Britain became rich under Roman rule for the invaders mined lead, tin in Cornwall, iron, silver and copper. The remains of a Roman gold mine have been unearthed in Wales. The kilns used by the Romans were advanced for the time and there have been frequent finds of pottery on their military sites throughout Britain. Recent excavations at Fishbourne in Sussex have revealed a Roman palace.

Ancient Rome

ROMANS IN BRITAIN
SOME IMPORTANT SITES
Some main Roman roads in Britain

Housesteads

Only example of a Roman hospital in Britain and a toilet with a flushing tank.

Vindolanda

Well-preserved fort where Roman sandals and writing tablets were found.

Chester

People can walk on ancient Roman walls.

Wroxeter

The old Roman fort Virconium — A military tombstone found over the grave of a Roman soldier.

Bath

A Roman health center was built around the natural hot spring at Bath.

Watling St. – probably Britain's earliest Roman road.
Dere St. – the main supply road for the frontier armies.

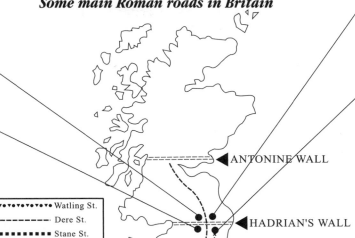

Watling St.
Dere St.
Stane St.
Ermine St.
Fosse Way

Manchester
Chester
Bath
Exeter

ANTONINE WALL

HADRIAN'S WALL

Most Roman remains are found near their widespread road network.

Chesters

Best preserved remains of cavalry fort.

Corbridge

Best preserved Roman granaries.

Thetford

The "Thetford treasure" discovered in 1979 is one of the largest finds of Roman gold and silver artifacts.

Sischester

Roman walls and a circular embankment (the remains of an amphitheater) are visible.

In January 2000, Britains weekly *Telegraph* reported as a result of floods, an old Roman harbor 240 km up the River Severn had been exposed to archaeologists.

Activity Box

1. How many years since the "Thetford treasure" was found?

   _____

2. Which road leads to one of the first Roman naval bases? _____

3. Which road goes from Exeter to Lincoln?

   _____

4. What was the Roman name for Wroxeter?

   _____

5. Why was Bath (Aquae Sulis) so important?

   _____

6. Which road goes up to the Antonine Wall?

   _____

7. What is an artifact?

   _____

8. What was stored in granaries?

   _____

9. Use an atlas and find out in which county you would find Dover. _____

10. How many sites are shown on or near Hadrian's Wall?

    _____

THE FIRST EMPEROR – AUGUSTUS

While most of the Empire was shared between Octavian and Antony, their ally Lepidus, who formed a triumvirate with them, was given control of part of the north African region of the Empire. Once he was firmly established in the west, Octavian prepared to attack Antony, who had befriended Cleopatra, the queen of Egypt, a woman Rome did not trust.

After the battle of Actium, Antony and Cleopatra fled, and the struggle for power in the civil wars ended when they both committed suicide in Egypt when Octavian invaded the country on the Nile. For many years, Egypt then became the main provider of corn for Rome.

During his reign, Augustus added new provinces to the Empire and new cities were built. He made changes to the army, the tax system, the judiciary and Roman coinage. This laid a solid foundation for the Rome of the future. Augustus was a brilliant politician for, unlike some later emperors, he did not abuse the supreme power he wielded and so strengthened the position of the emperor. Rome was ruled by emperors for the next 400 years.

A temple built to remember Augustus and his wife, Livia, can still be visited by tourists in France to this day.

The emperor created a group of firefighters called "vigils," who were freed slaves. Perhaps our word "vigilant" has the same Latin root.

During the reign of Augustus the arts flourished in Rome and the writings of poets such as Virgil and Horace were popular with the rich and powerful citizens.

THE FIRST EMPEROR – AUGUSTUS

Octavian, Julius Caesar's adopted son, and Caesar's friend, Mark Antony, defeated Caesar's murderers, Brutus and Cassius, at the battle of Philippi in 42 B.C., two years after Caesar's assassination. Octavian then ruled over the Western Empire and Antony the East, but later they quarreled over the division of power and Octavian's victory at the sea battle of Actium in 31 B.C. left him as the sole ruler.

He was granted the title of Augustus ("the dignified one") by the Senate and became the first official emperor of Rome in 27 B.C. He had brought an end to the civil wars following the death of Julius Caesar and he reigned for over 40 years.

Under the Emperor Augustus, Rome became one of the greatest cities of all time. He divided the city into fourteen administrative areas similar to our city councils today. Each area was controlled by a magistrate. Augustus also organized the world's first fire brigade, using slaves to fight fires, and a police force to control a growing crime problem in the city streets. To prevent the Tiber from flooding the city he widened part of the river and had it dredged to remove mud and rubbish. He also ensured that the monthly distribution of free corn to the city's poor citizens was continued. Many of Rome's buildings were faced with expensive marble and Augustus boasted that he "found Rome brick and left it marble." He built new aqueducts and repaired old ones, and the huge sewer known as the Cloaca Maxima was also repaired during his reign (27 B.C.–14 A.D.). In 14 A.D. Augustus died and Tiberius succeeded him as emperor.

Augustus's statue—made by a sculptor during the emperor's reign.

Activity Box

1. In what year was Julius Caesar murdered?

   _____

2. What do you think was the greatest achievement by Augustus?

   _____

   Why?_____

   _____

3. Why did Octavian and Antony meet in the battle of Actium?

   _____

   _____

   _____

4. How often was free corn given out to the poor?

   _____

5. How long had the civil wars lasted after Caesar's death?

   _____

6. Why was a police force needed?

   _____

7. Why did Augustus widen the River Tiber?

   _____

8. Which word in the notes above means "costly"?

   _____

ENEMIES OF ROME – HANNIBAL

As the city of Rome spread its influence throughout Italy, the western parts of the Mediterranean were under the control of the Carthaginians, people from the north African coastal city of Carthage. Carthage had been founded in the eighth century B.C. by the Phoenicians, a trading nation from the Middle East. When the trading interests of Carthage and Rome clashed, a series of wars known as the Punic wars (Punic – Latin for Phoenicians) broke out between the two powerful nations.

According to one writer called Polybius, Hannibal crossed the Alps with 90,000 troops and 12,000 cavalry, but these figures are regarded as too high by historians. Only a few of Hannibal's elephants survived the rugged mountain terrain and the icy conditions.

After razing Carthage to the ground, the Romans plowed the land with salt so crops could never grow there again.

Note:

Before they write their description, remind students of the intense cold, the problems of taking elephants and cavalry horses across mountains and a river, and the attacks by fierce tribes.

ENEMIES OF ROME – HANNIBAL

After losing the islands of Sicily, Corsica and Sardinia to the Romans, the Carthaginians from the north African city of Carthage needed to extend their empire. They invaded and conquered Spain in the second century B.C. Spain was a source of silver, which could be used to pay tribute to Rome, and a country where mercenaries (soldiers who fight for anyone in return for money) could be found for Carthaginian armies.

Their commanding general in Spain was a brilliant 29-year-old military leader called Hannibal, who despised the Romans. During the second Punic war, Roman warships controlled the Mediterranean Sea, so Hannibal surprised the Romans by marching through northern Spain in 218 B.C. with over 35,000 men and 38 war elephants—used to break up enemy battle formations. After ferrying the elephants across the River Rhone on rafts, he crossed the Alps in winter and marched into Italy. His army was now reduced to about 25,000 men because of the intense cold and attacks by fierce mountain tribes, but it was increased to around 40,000 by enlisting Gauls, traditional enemies of Rome.

Hannibal's army won battle after battle and killed 50,000 legionaries at Cannae in 216 B.C. Though he never conquered Rome itself, Hannibal fought in Italy for 16 years and suffered no heavy defeats. Being unsuccessful against Hannibal in Italy, the Romans invaded and conquered Spain and then attacked Carthage. When they destroyed Carthage in 146 B.C., after over 100 years of war between the two nations, Rome became the most powerful nation in the Mediterranean region.

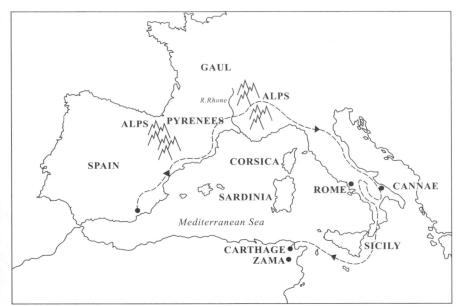

Hannibal returned to Carthage but was finally defeated at Zama in 202 B.C. by the military commander Scipio. Hannibal was on the run from the Romans for years until he poisoned himself in 182 B.C.

Activity Box

Hannibal's crossing of the Alps is one of history's greatest military strategies. Imagine you're an ancient chronicler with his army. Describe the crossing.

ENEMIES OF ROME
– ALARIC

Several Roman emperors allowed some tribes of barbarians (people so described by Rome because they lived outside the frontiers of the Roman Empire) inside their boundaries and bribed them to keep out other enemies of Rome. Though in later years Alaric's services were not used, he still demanded payment, but this was refused by the Senate.

Stilicho, the great military leader who was part Vandal by birth, was master of the Roman legions in the Western Empire. He had suggested Alaric should be used to suppress troublesome tribes in Gaul, but Honorius accused Stilicho of treason and executed him.

Barbarian invasions by the Vandals or Suebi saw the confiscation of land or property, but the Visigoths sought acceptance by the Romans and the opportunity to settle on land of their own. Alaric attacked Rome in 408 A.D. and 409 A.D., but accepted huge ransoms to end both sieges.

When Alaric sacked Rome in 410 A.D., the Romans abandoned Britain in the same year. Their legions were needed to defend Rome and its shrinking Empire from constant barbarian attacks.

Alaric was buried, with weapons and armor, in the bed of a stream which was temporarily diverted. The stream was then allowed to flow along its old course again and the grave site was buried. Roman prisoners who had dug the grave were killed to keep its location a secret.

ENEMIES OF ROME – ALARIC

Alaric hoped to become a military officer in the Roman army. He was chief of a tribe called the Visigoths from the kingdom of Thrace. Alaric had helped one Roman emperor crush a rebellion, but a later emperor declared that there was no longer any need for Alaric's services, so the Visigoth leader decided to create a new kingdom as a homeland for his people. He attacked and looted many cities in Greece but eventually fled from a Roman army. Alaric had invaded Italy twice before but now decided to attack Rome. After several unsuccessful assaults on the city, Alaric spent two years trying to negotiate with the young Emperor Honorius who, frightened by the Visigoth invasion, had moved his court to the fortified city of Ravenna on Italy's east coast, where he eventually died. Alaric finally lost patience and in 310 A.D. his warriors plundered Rome, though he spared the churches. He then established a kingdom in northern Italy.

A Gothic Warrior

The sacking of Rome by a barbarian force was a warning to people throughout the Empire and as a result, the Romans in North Africa cut off supplies of corn to Rome. Alaric had planned to invade the island of Sicily and Rome's North African provinces to get the grain ships sailing again. However, many of his ships were wrecked in a storm and most of his warriors were drowned. Not long after this disaster Alaric died, possibly from a fever, and his army retreated to northern Italy.

Activity Box

1. Why were grain supplies from Africa stopped?

   _____

2. Why didn't Alaric invade Sicily?

   _____

   _____

3. Why did Alaric flee from Greece?

   _____

4. Why do you think Alaric would have been annoyed that a later emperor no longer needed his services?

   _____

   _____

5. Why do you think Alaric spared Rome's churches from destruction?

   _____

Clues

Across

3. Fighting body of men
5. Ran away
7. A realm
9. The Roman world
13. Plundered
14. Assisted
16. A couple
17. Home of the Visigoths
18. An ailment suffered by Alaric
19. Group of fighting men
22. A revolt
23. Provided corn
25. Describes the Emperor Honorius

Down

1. Necessity
2. Center of the Empire
4. Withdrew
6. Alaric intended to attack this island
8. Relating to the army
10. Strengthened against attacks
11. It sank many of Alaric's ships
12. They carried grain
15. Honorius was one
20. Ravenna is in this country
21. Supplied by Rome's African provinces
24. Corn supplies were _____ off

THE FALL OF ROME

Though corruption and civil unrest over burdensome taxes probably helped to bring about Rome's decline, the most telling factor was the barbarian invasions. The Visigoths under Alaric plundered Rome for three days in 410 A.D. and from this time Rome's greatness began to collapse. The Visigoths also invaded Spain but withdrew to Gaul and established a capital at the present city of Toulouse.

The Vandals and Goths originated in southern Scandinavia. After conquering Rome's North African provinces and Carthage in 439 A.D., the Vandals invaded Italy and sacked Rome in 455 A.D.

In many regions overrun by the barbarians, the local leaders lived as before, for they were needed to assist in running the new kingdoms.

Many barbarians such as the Vandals were savage warriors who wanted to wipe out all traces of the Romans. Other tribes wanted to preserve Roman buildings but did not have the expertise to maintain them. Over the years of barbarian attacks, the population of Rome fell from 1,000,000 to about 25,000.

While the Western Empire was the scene for years of power struggles among Germanic kings, the Eastern Empire was ruled from the city of Constantinople and called the Byzantine empire after the fall of the Western Empire. Constantinople was founded by the first Christian emperor, Constantine, in 330 A.D. as his new capital. Many eastern emperors were capable rulers and one, Justinian, even won back some of the lost western provinces. The Eastern Empire was rich and could afford strong armies which resisted the Germanic tribes and the Persians.

THE FALL OF ROME

Over hundreds of years, the Romans had to repel attacks by barbarian hordes. The Empire was so large it became more and more difficult to defend and was eventually divided into the Eastern and Western empires.

Roman frontiers suffered constant raids and invasions by barbarian tribes like the Vandals who, aided by the Alans and Suebi, invaded Spain in 409 A.D. The Vandals then conquered the Roman provinces in North Africa in 439 A.D. and in 455 A.D., still led by their King Gaiseric, they sacked and plundered Rome itself for two weeks. In other parts of the Empire, the Angles, Jutes and Saxons from northern Europe invaded Britain from 449 A.D. after the Roman

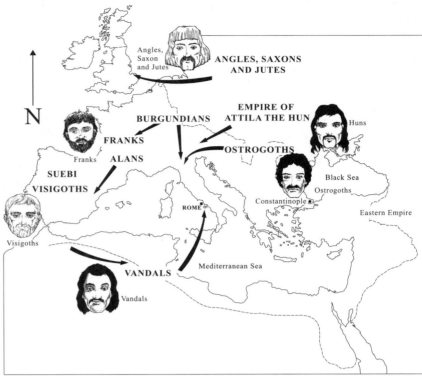

A Hun Warrior

legions were withdrawn from Britain to defend Rome. The Franks, who gave us the name France, and other Germanic tribes had invaded the Roman province of Gaul in 406 A.D. and the Visigoths under Alaric attacked Rome several times between 400 and 410 A.D. The Ostrogoths had migrated westwards from Asia in 370 A.D. to escape from the Huns, the most feared invaders of all. Under their leader, Attila, the Huns invaded Italy in 452 A.D. and it was only negotiations by Pope Leo I that saved Rome from further destruction. Attila died the following year and the empire of the Huns disintegrated. Later that century, Ostrogoths invaded Italy under their king, Theoderic, and overran the whole Italian peninsula.

Some historians believe that the Roman legions in these desperate times were not the disciplined, loyal armies of the early years of the Empire. Many legionaries were mercenaries, paid foreign soldiers from conquered nations, who did not have the same loyalty to Rome as her native sons.

Activity Box

Write a few sentences about one of the barbarian leaders—Alaric, Attila the Hun, Theoderic, or Gaiseric. Use any available reference resources.

_____

_____

_____

_____

THE LEGACY OF ROME

The Romans left us a legacy of ideas and our world today would be a different one had they not lived in it.

Law

Roman laws form the basis of the legal systems of many modern nations.

Roads

The legions constructed thousands of kilometers of roads throughout the Empire. Some are still used as a base for modern roads.

Towns

The inhabitants of much of Europe were rural tribes or wandering nomads and the Romans introduced them to the advantages of urban living. Many modern cities are sited on old Roman army camps or on excellent townsites selected by the Romans (e.g., London, Paris).

Buildings

Many modern structures like the White House (Washington), the Arc de Triomphe (Paris) and the British Museum (London) are copies of Roman styles of building. The Pantheon, a temple to all the Roman gods, is still one of the largest single-span domes in the world. The Romans built the first multi-story buildings, the forerunners of our apartments. Roman builders first used cement and later, around 200 B.C., developed the use of concrete. Though they didn't invent the arch, Roman builders also mastered the difficult techniques for building stone arches.

Calendar

The divisions into months and weeks and the names of the months come from the Romans (e.g., Janus—January, Augustus–August).

Language

Over half of the words we use in the English language are derived from Latin, the language of the Romans. The languages of Spain, Portugal, Italy and France are even more closely linked to the Latin language.

Religion

The emperor Constantine made Christianity the official religion of the Empire and today the Pope, the head of the Roman Catholic church, lives in Rome and has millions of followers.

Many of the things we take for granted today were first introduced by the Romans—a postal delivery service, a fire brigade, scissors, door keys, weight scales, theater curtains, milestones, glass windows, hospitals, central heating and even the letters in the words you are reading now.

Activity Suggestion

Create your own page titled "The Legacy of Rome" and use cut-out pictures from papers and magazines or your own diagrams to illustrate some of the above ideas we have inherited from the Romans.

ACTIVITY 1 – ROMAN QUIZ

1. Chariot with two horses
   - (a) Duoga ☐
   - (b) Biga ☐
   - (c) Quadriga ☐

2. Tool for scraping dirt off skin
   - (a) Toga ☐
   - (b) Bulla ☐
   - (c) Strigil ☐

3. Pottery jar for storing wine
   - (a) Aqueduct ☐
   - (b) Insula ☐
   - (c) Amphora ☐

4. Public baths
   - (a) Thermae ☐
   - (b) Fresco ☐
   - (c) Mosaic ☐

5. Large catapult for sieges
   - (a) Toga ☐
   - (b) Vallum ☐
   - (c) Onager ☐

6. Block of apartments
   - (a) Atrium ☐
   - (b) Insula ☐
   - (c) Villa ☐

7. City's central meeting place
   - (a) Consul ☐
   - (b) Atrium ☐
   - (c) Forum ☐

8. Conquered land
   - (a) Province ☐
   - (b) Scabbard ☐
   - (c) Republic ☐

9. Fighting men
   - (a) Quarries ☐
   - (b) Senators ☐
   - (c) Gladiators ☐

10. Roman robe
    - (a) Onager ☐
    - (b) Toga ☐
    - (c) Fresco ☐

11. Military officer
    - (a) Senator ☐
    - (b) Brazier ☐
    - (c) Centurion ☐

12. Battering ram
    - (a) Ballista ☐
    - (b) Onager ☐
    - (c) Aries ☐

13. Water carrying system
    - (a) Insulae ☐
    - (b) Denarius ☐
    - (c) Aqueduct ☐

14. A stabbing sword
    - (a) Gladius ☐
    - (b) Brazier ☐
    - (c) Mosaic ☐

15. Wall painting on wet plaster.
    - (a) Mithras ☐
    - (b) Fresco ☐
    - (c) Atrium ☐

16. Fire holder
    - (a) Brazier ☐
    - (b) Forum ☐
    - (c) Strigil ☐

17. Room in a villa
    - (a) Vallum ☐
    - (b) Artifact ☐
    - (c) Atrium ☐

18. Army unit
    - (a) Region ☐
    - (b) Visor ☐
    - (c) Legion ☐

19. Foreign soldiers
    - (a) Auxiliaries ☐
    - (c) Centurions ☐
    - (c) Quarries ☐

20. Tile patterns
    - (a) Togas ☐
    - (b) Mosaics ☐
    - (c) Thermae ☐

21. Chariot-racing stadium
    - (a) Amphorae ☐
    - (b) Consul ☐
    - (c) Circus ☐

22. Roman coin
    - (a) Domus ☐
    - (b) Denarius ☐
    - (c) Goth ☐

23. French tribes
    - (a) Onagers ☐
    - (b) Patricians ☐
    - (c) Gauls ☐

24. Governing body
    - (a) Forum ☐
    - (b) Senate ☐
    - (c) Colosseum ☐

25. A house
    - (a) Domus ☐
    - (b) Papyrus ☐
    - (c) Forum ☐

26. Chariot team
    - (a) Yellows ☐
    - (b) Pinks ☐
    - (c) Greens ☐

27. Brother of Romulus
    - (a) Domus ☐
    - (b) Remus ☐
    - (c) Visor ☐

28. Color of stripes on a senator's robe
    - (a) Purple ☐
    - (b) Red ☐
    - (c) Yellow ☐

29. Teacher of public speaking
    - (a) Centaur ☐
    - (b) Amphora ☐
    - (c) Rhetor ☐

30. An eagle standard
    - (a) Aquila ☐
    - (b) Insula ☐
    - (c) Ballista ☐

31. Highest political position
    - (a) Tribune ☐
    - (b) Senator ☐
    - (c) Consul ☐

32. Large country house with estate
    - (a) Atrium ☐
    - (b) Villa ☐
    - (c) Vallum ☐

33. Curve on Roman road
    - (a) Ballista ☐
    - (b) Strigil ☐
    - (c) Camber ☐

34. Celtic tribe
    - (a) Iceni ☐
    - (b) Patricians ☐
    - (c) Consuls ☐

35. Roman shield
    - (a) Hasta ☐
    - (b) Scutum ☐
    - (c) Gladius ☐

36. Battle formation
    - (a) Ballista ☐
    - (b) Testudo ☐
    - (c) Deity ☐

37. Farming tool
    - (a) Scythe ☐
    - (b) Gladius ☐
    - (c) Hasta ☐

38. God of war
    - (a) Mercury ☐
    - (b) Ceres ☐
    - (c) Mars ☐

39. Roman spear
    - (a) Centaur ☐
    - (b) Hasta ☐
    - (c) Fresco ☐

40. Old name for France
    - (a) Britannia ☐
    - (b) Pompeii ☐
    - (c) Gaul ☐

ACTIVITY 2 – ROMAN COINS

Roman coins had different values in relation to each other in the Imperial and Republic years. The metals they were made of also changed throughout the history of Rome. The coins in this activity were in use from the first to the third century A.D. Each coin had the emperor's head on it to prove it was genuine.

Aureus (aurei) – Rome's first gold coin	25 denarii to an aureus
Denarius (denarii) – Main silver coin	4 sestertii to a denarius
Sestertius (sestertii) – Brass coin	A dupondius is worth $\frac{1}{2}$ a sestertius
Dupondius (dupondii) – Brass coin	4 asses to a sestertius
As (asses) – Copper coin	2 semis to an as
Semi (semis) – Bronze coin	4 quadrans to an as
Quadran (quadrans) – Copper coin	

Activity Box

Use the above information to solve the problems.

(a) A Senator buys rolls of silk for 4 aurei or _____ denarii.

(b) A patrician buys a painting for 12 sestertii or _____ asses.

(c) A centurion has his gladius repaired for 32 quadrans or _____ sestertii.

(d) A legionary buys a helmet for 20 dupondii or _____ asses.

(e) A Roman trader sells wine for 8 aurei or _____ sestertii.

(f) A Roman potter makes an amphora for 10 asses or _____ quadrans.

(g) A consul pays 10 aurei or _____ sestertii for a chariot.

(h) A tribune wins 150 denarii or _____ aurei gambling at the circus.

(i) A farmer buys a new scythe for one denarius or _____ semis.

(j) A Roman slave spends 5 sestertii or _____ quadrans on grapes for his master.

(k) A charioteer spends 2 aurei or _____ dupondii on food for his horses.

(l) A rich Roman mother spends 3 aurei or _____ denarii on a model chariot for her son.

(m) A merchant pays 300 sestertii or _____ aurei on taxes for imported goods.

(n) A school student spends 6 semis or _____ asses for a stylus.

(o) A Roman priest buys a temple statue for 600 denarii or _____ aurei.

ACTIVITY 3 – TIME LINE GAME

Toss the dice and then move the number of spaces shown. The counters move in an counterclockwise direction as did the horses in chariot races at the circus. When landing on an instruction space, **the instruction is read aloud** and then the necessary move made.

START

FINISH

Mythical founding of Rome in 753 B.C.
Go forward 3 spaces

In 510 B.C. Rome became a republic
Go forward 2 spaces

↓

↓

Hannibal crossed the Alps in 218 B.C.
Go back 2 spaces

↓

215 B.C. Restriction on amount of jewelry worn by women
Go back 1 space

146 B.C. Rome destroys Carthage
Go forward 2 spaces

Julius Caesar's Julian calendar has 365 days in a year in 45 B.C.
Go forward 1 space

↓

44 – 30 B.C. Civil wars in Rome after murder of Julius Caesar
Go back 5 spaces

43 A.D. Britain invaded during reign of Claudius
Go forward 6 spaces

60 A.D. Rebellion of Iceni leader called Boudica
Go back 3 spaces

64 A.D. Christians blamed by Emperor Nero for huge fire in Rome.
Go back 4 spaces

166 A.D. Roman armies bring plague from Eastern Empire.
Go back 5 spaces

197 A.D. Roman troops could now marry.
Go forward 2 spaces

270 A.D. Emperor Aurelian built the Aurelian defense wall around Rome.
Go forward 2 spaces

↑

303 A.D. Great persecution of Christians.
Go back 9 spaces

406 A.D. River Rhine freezes over. Goths cross into Roman territory
Go back 9 spaces

410 A.D. Legions withdrawn from England to defend Rome.
Go forward 4 spaces

410 A.D. Visigoth leader Alaric plunders Rome.
Go back 4 spaces

↑

439 A.D. The Vandals conquer Roman Africa.
Go back 6 spaces

←

476 A.D. Fall of the Western Empire to the Barbarians.
Go back 6 spaces

1453 A.D. Eastern Empire falls to The Ottoman Turks.
Go back 6 spaces

ACTIVITY 4 – COORDINATES

A Roman battle (2 persons)

TT — Trireme (warship with 3 banks of oars on each side)

QQQ — Quinquereme (warship with 5 banks of oars on each side)

B — Ballista (bolt-firing machine)

O — Onager (catapult for hurling rocks)

A — Aries (battering ram)

S — Siege tower

Follow the steps in the procedure below.

1. Each partner uses the blank 10x10 square on page 107.

2. The players set their own battle scene with the same number of war machines as the example.

3. Player "A" then gives a coordinate reading, say F4, and player "B" checks on his sheet and says "a miss" if player "A" is unsuccessful. If player "A" says H7, as on the example, player "B" would say "damage on my trireme" and put a cross through H7. Player "A" would then have a bonus turn (after a "hit") and would try to sink the trireme with another "hit."

4. When a player has a turn they must place a dot in their nominated coordinate reading so they know which readings they have used.

5. The winner is the one who destroys the other player's war machines first.

Note: The horizontal line must be read first (for example, D6, A9).

The game could be played over the period of time the Romans are being studied as students complete a worksheet. Time limits could be in place—say 10 minutes—with the player destroying most enemy war machines being declared the winner.

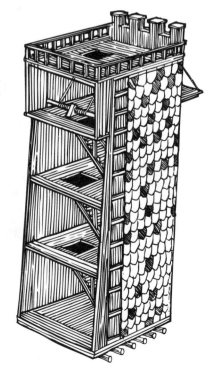

Ancient Rome

ACTIVITY 4 – COORDINATES

	A	B	C	D	E	F	G	H	I	J
x										
ix										
viii										
vii										
vi										
v										
iv										
iii										
ii										
i										

ROME – ANSWERS

Page 7
Foundation of Rome (1)
1. fertile farmland
2. Tarquin
3. Citizens elect their rulers
4. South
5. Middle East and Britain
6. becoming powerful, fertile land, growing population
7. Teacher Check

Page 9
Foundation of Rome (2)
8. Macedonia, Greece
   Cyrenaica, Libya
   Cappadocia, Turkey
   Gallia, France
   Britannia, Britain
   Hispania, Spain
   Numidia, Algeria
   Thracia, Bulgaria
9. Teacher Check

Page 11
Romulus and Remus
1. Romulus
2. Numitor
3. Amulius
4. Answers may vary
5. killing his brother's sons
6. Answers may vary
7. (a) furious (b) banished (c) slew
8. Romulus and Remus
9. ordered, commanded
10. great uncle

Page 13
Romulus and Remus

Page 15
Destruction of Pompeii
1. 62 A.D.
2. because it is so well preserved
3. 10%
4. an eye-witness account
5. to dig out valuables and personal possessions
6. poisonous fumes
7. Teacher check
8. (a) inhabitants (b) shrill (c) poisonous (d) site (e) buried

Page 15
Evacuations at Pompeii
Teacher Check

Page 19
Roman Legions (1)
Teacher check

Page 21
Roman Legions (2)
1. The Roman army was made up of volunteers.
2. they were given gold
3. training, organizations and equipment
4. false
5. tribal warrior leaders
6. foot soldiers
7. crushed, humiliating
8. 100 years
9. Roman soldiers
10. marching long distances with heavy loads

Page 23
Roman Legions (3)
1. Answers may vary
2. Sickness was treated in the home.

Page 25
Roman Legions (4)
1. The soldiers and the craftsmen.
2. They were straight.
3. Watling Street.

Page 29
Roman Slaves (1)
Answers will vary

Page 31
Roman Slaves (2)
Answers will vary

Page 33
Roman Slaves – Spartacus
1. 71 B.C.
2. Southwest
3. (a) vast (b) assembled
4. auxilia
5. Tacitus
6. Return to their homelands.
7. Answers may vary
8. The Alps
9. fear
10. Answers may vary

Page 35
Government – The Republic
1. Patricians
2. 244 years
3. Tribunes
4. consuls
5. Augustus
6. laws
7. senate
8. a dictator

ROME – ANSWERS

Page 37
Roman Gods and Goddesses (1)

2. (1) Saturn (2) flowers (3) carried
   (4) underworld (5) angry (6) barren
   (7) search (8) journey (9) ailing
   (10) took (11) taught
   (12) agriculture (13) persuaded
   (14) mother (15) eating (16) seeds
   (17) third (18) delighted (19) return
   (20) fertile

Page 39
Roman Gods and Goddesses (2)

Teacher check

Page 41
Roman Gods and Goddesses (3)

Teacher check

Page 45
Roman Life – Homes (2)

1. they couldn't afford houses
2. the climate there was cold and damp
3. a slave
4. oil lamps
5. mosaic
6. the atrium
7. huts
8. There was a shortage of land.
9. brazier
10. privacy

Page 47
Roman Life – Homes (3)

Teacher check

Page 51
Roman Life – Food (2)

Teacher Check

Page 53
Roman Life – Food (3)

bread, cheese, chicken, dates, eggs,
fish, grapes, honey, mushrooms, nuts,
olives, pork, porridge, prawns,
vegetables, venison

Page 55
Roman Life – Education

1. Answers may vary
2. abacus
3. to avoid the heat
4. public speaking
5. Answers may vary

Page 57
Roman Life – Public Baths

Answers may vary, e.g.,

Similarities	Differences
e.g., Both have cafes	e.g., The Romans sold wine.
1. Both have gardens	1. The Roman bath house had a theater
2. Both have public toilets	2. The Roman bath house had a library
3. Both have heated pools	3. Roman baths often free to the poor
4. Both have cold pools	4. Roman baths employed slaves
5. Both poor and rich use them	5. Roman bathers used strigils

Page 59
Roman Life – Entertainment (1)

1. Juvenal
2. to gain votes and keep control
3. successful gladiators
4. noon
5. animals
6. gladiatorial schools
7. Answers may vary
8. arena
9. a retiarius
10. Christians
11. Answers may vary

Page 61
Roman Life – Entertainment (2)

Page 63
Roman Life – Entertainment (3)

1. (1) origins (2) earlier
   (3) performing (4) actors
   (5) presented (6) masks
   (7) characters (8) women (9) heroes
   (10) mouth (11) talk (12) enjoyed
   (13) wealthier (14) slaves
   (15) audiences (16) comedy
   (17) music (18) actor (19) legendary
   (20) instruments (21) horns
   (22) speaking (23) afford (24) poets
   (25) entertain

Page 67
Farming

1. women
2. olives and vines
3. sheep
4. with animal manure
5. Answers may vary

Page 69
Farming – Tools (1)

Teacher check

Page 71
Farming – Tools (2)

Teacher check

Page 73
Trade

1. to avoid the winter storms
2. One was found near the Thames river
3. pirates
4. reflecting mirrors
5. they didn't have compasses
6. Answers may vary

ROME – ANSWERS

Page 75
Roman Technology – Aqueducts

1. to catch sand and sediment
2. to use the pull of gravity
3. by the diameter of their water pipe
4. sewers
5. wells, springs, streams
6. drought
7. Tiber River, sea
8. arches
9. polluted water
10. underground pipes

Page 77
Roman Technology

(a) (1) support (2) beds (3) enclosure (4) circles (5) clay (6) water (7) pumped (8) dug
(b) (1) mixture (2) sand (3) Romans (4) Timber (5) support (6) hardened (7) faced (8) bricks
(c) (1) invent (2) strong (3) stones (4) wedges (5) side (6) frame (7) keystone (8) top

Page 79
Roman Women

1. made of silk
2. the right to vote, to become a magistrate, the rights over children
3. Answers may vary
4.

	F		F	E	W			H	
	L			O	F	T	E	N	
	O	I	L		O			L	
	U		C	L	A	S	P	S	
	R	I	C	H		I		C	
			A			M		E	
	W	L	O	T	I	O	N	S	
S	I	L	K		L		T		
	G		S	L	A	V	E	S	
A	S	S			R		D		

Page 81
Roman Life – Language

1. beast 2. December 3. martial
4. vigilant 5. pedal 6. gladiolus
7. navy 8. domestic 9. tepid
10. volume 11. valediction 12. salary
13. prefect 14. aquiline 15. principal
16. marital

Page 83
Roman Life – Numbers

1. (a) $10+1 = 11$ (A)
   (b) $50+10 = 60$ (A)
   (C) $10+10+10+ (10-1) = 39$ (A & S)
   (d) $1,000+100+100 = 1,200$ (A)
   (e) $100-10 = 90$ (S)
   (f) $50-10 = 40$ (S)
   (g) $100+50+10 = 160$ (A)
   (h) $500+100+100 = 700$ (A)
   (i) $1,000+100+50+(5-1) = 1,154$ (A&S)
   (j) $1,000+500+100+100+100 = 1,800$ (A)
2. (a) 50,000 (b) 100,000 (c) 6,000
   (d) 16,000 (e) 600,000 (f) 1,000,000
   (g) 60,000 (h) 90,000 (i) 70,000
   (j) 55,000 (k) 10,000 (l) 20,000

Page 87
Romans in Britain

Page 89
Romans in Britain – Hadrian

1. Trajan
2. Germanic
3. people have taken the stones
4. turf
5. forced payments to ruling nations
6. Irish and North seas
7. local Britons
8. he had arranged a treaty with the Scots

Page 91
Romans in Britain – Boudica

1. (1) tribe (2) eastern (3) army (4) Roman (5) spare (6) cooperated (7) liberate (8) invaders (9) troops (10) governor (11) equipped (12) organized (13) experienced (14) javelins (15) drew (16) swords (17) shields (18) rout (19) fled (20) slew
2. (a) tall (b) terrifying (c) fierce (d) harsh
3. 14
4. rout
5. they killed women and children
6. liberate
7. military/general
8. Iceni
9. false

Page 93
Romans in Britain – Some Important Sites

1. Teacher check
2. Watling Street
3. Fosse Way
4. Virconium
5. it was a natural spring
6. Dere Street
7. an object from the past
8. grain/corn
9. Kent
10. 4

ROME – ANSWERS

Page 95
The First Emperor – Augustus
1. 44 B.C.
2. Answers may vary
3. They fought over the division of power
4. every month
5. 13 years (44–31 B.C.)
6. crime was increasing
7. to prevent flooding
7. expensive

Page 99
Enemies of Rome – Alaric
1. Rome was attacked
2. Many of his ships were destroyed in a storm
3. he was attacked by a Roman army
4. because he had helped to crush a rebellion
5. Answers may vary

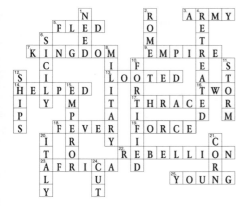

Page 104
Activity 2 – Roman Coins
(a) 100 (b) 48 (c) 2 (d) 40 (e) 800
(f) 40 (g) 1,000 (h) 6 (i) 32 (j) 80
(k) 400 (l) 75 (m) 3 (n) 3 (o) 24

Page 101
The Fall Of Rome
Teacher check

Page 103
Activity 1 – Roman Quiz
(1) b (2) c (3) c (4) a (5) c (6) b
(7) c (8) a (9) c (10) b (11) c (12) c
(13) c (14) a (15) b (16) a (17) c
(18) c (19) a (20) b (21) c (22) b
(23) c (24) b (25) a (26) c (27) b
(28) a (29) c (30) a (31) c (32) b
(33) c (34) a (35) b (36) b (37) a
(38) c (39) b (40) c

www.worldteacherspress.com ©World Teachers Press®